Karrie Ross

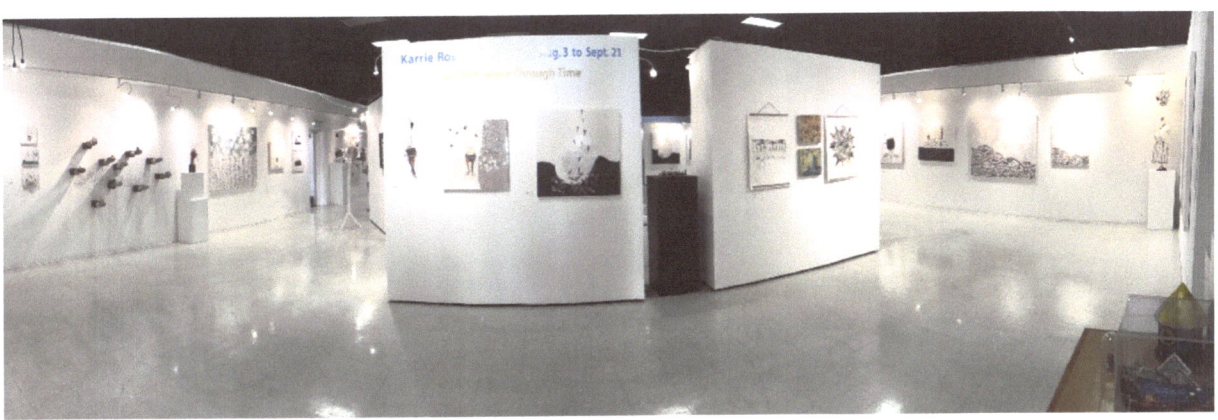

Blackboard Gallery,
Studio Channel Islands, Camarillo, California

Karrie Ross

2019 Blackboard Gallery, Camarillo, California

Copyright © 2019 Karrie Ross

All rights reserved. Except as permitted under U.S. Copyright Act of 1976, no part of this publication may be reproduced, distributed, or transmitted in any form or by any means, or stored in a database or retrieval system, without the prior written permission of the publisher.

Karrie Ross: 708 W. 140th Street, Gardena, CA 90247
Visit her website at www.KarrieRoss.com.

ISBN: 9781687391643

Image use is prohibited without written concent of the artist.

Printed in the United States of America

Book Design by Karrie Ross

Light & Space Through Time
2019

So many times we feel off balanced. That the flow of energy in our lives is not "right". We fight the feeling of "off" and yearn for the balance new perspectives bring.

A collaboration with nature: I direct my interests to seeking the answers for what it is like to "be human": I observe and listen to how people act. How they address their personal internal and community external interactions that create a story or unseen dialogue. My mixed-media art is constructed from the info I gather into physical form, applying juxtapositions intended to twist perception and make changes on a cellular level. Make them to look deeper and re-evaluate.

Exploring process in art making is exciting. The how to figuring-it-all-out part of Art. Paint—all things involved are considered. Chemistry, the time of year, temperature, cloud cover, moisture in the air, heating, air conditioning, paint dilution, type of paint, canvas, paper, panel, plexi, acrylic, oil, watercolor, all create rules that are not only risky but change with each painting. Creating a nature all it's own each time, each breath, just like life and as one progresses in explorations, and welcomes risk searching for the balance.

"Ross' art work is about the pursuit of answerable questions. She lives for them, and frames a life through the use of questions, rules and parameters."

~Robert S., reviewer

Karrie Ross
424-340-2000 landline
karrie@karrieross.com
www.karrieross.com

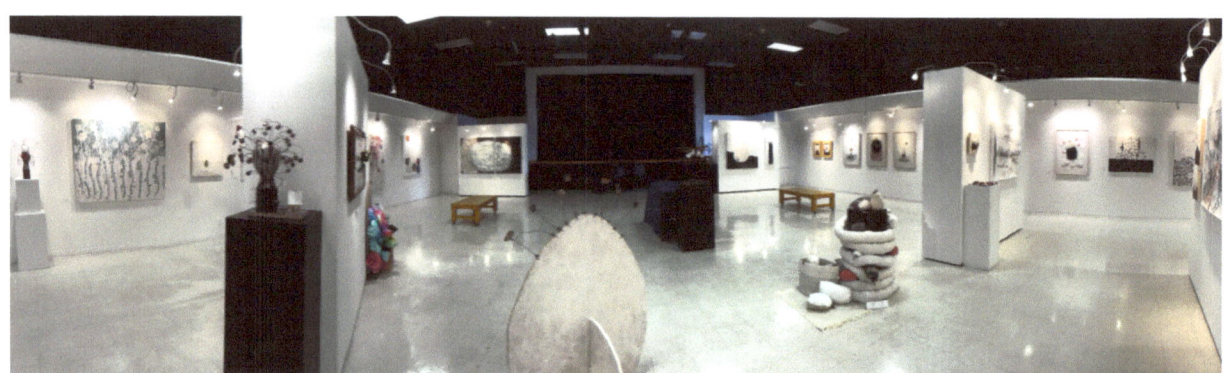
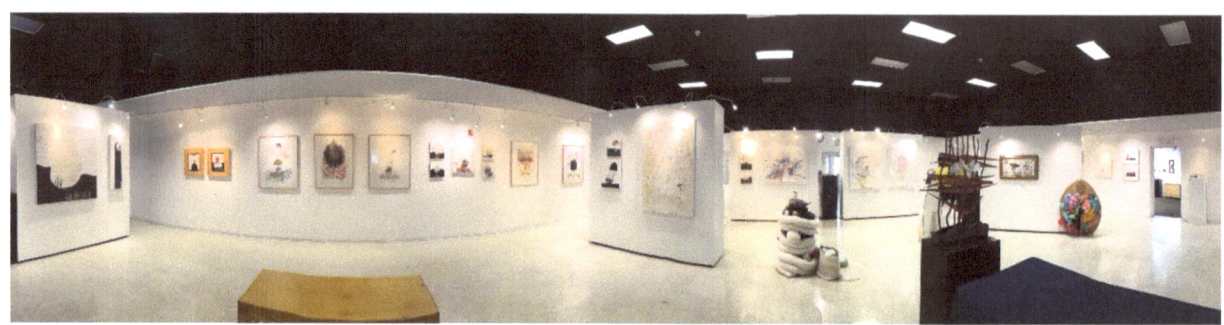
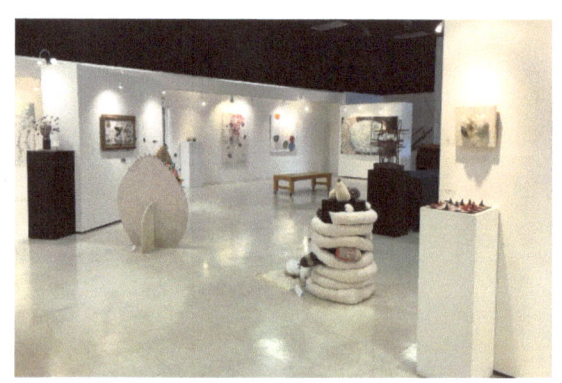

BlackBoard Gallery

Retrospective

Works from the last 2-3 years

2019

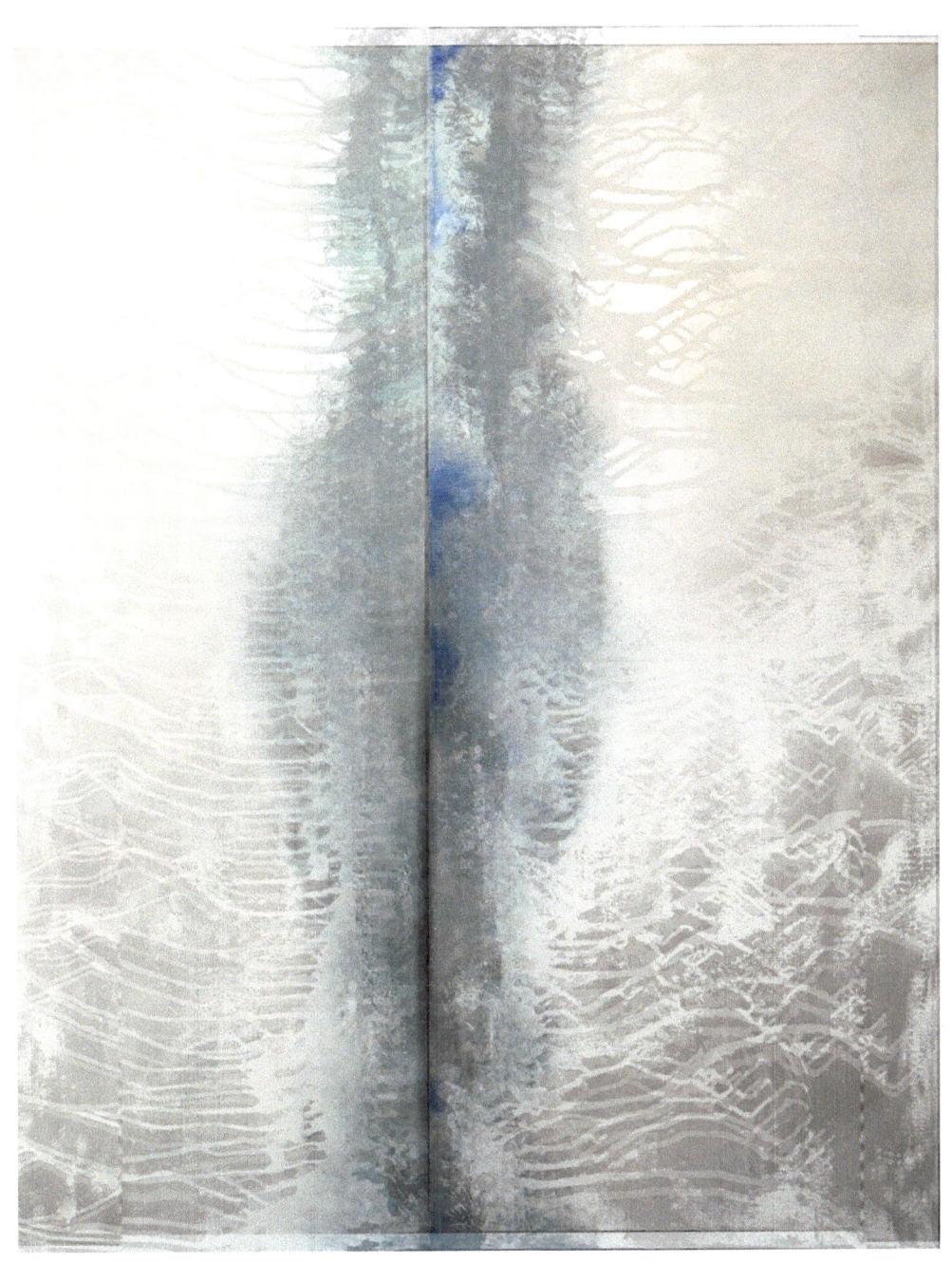

White Water Light #2; 2018; 72"x54"; two pieces; acrylic on canvas; (can be hung vertical or horizontal)

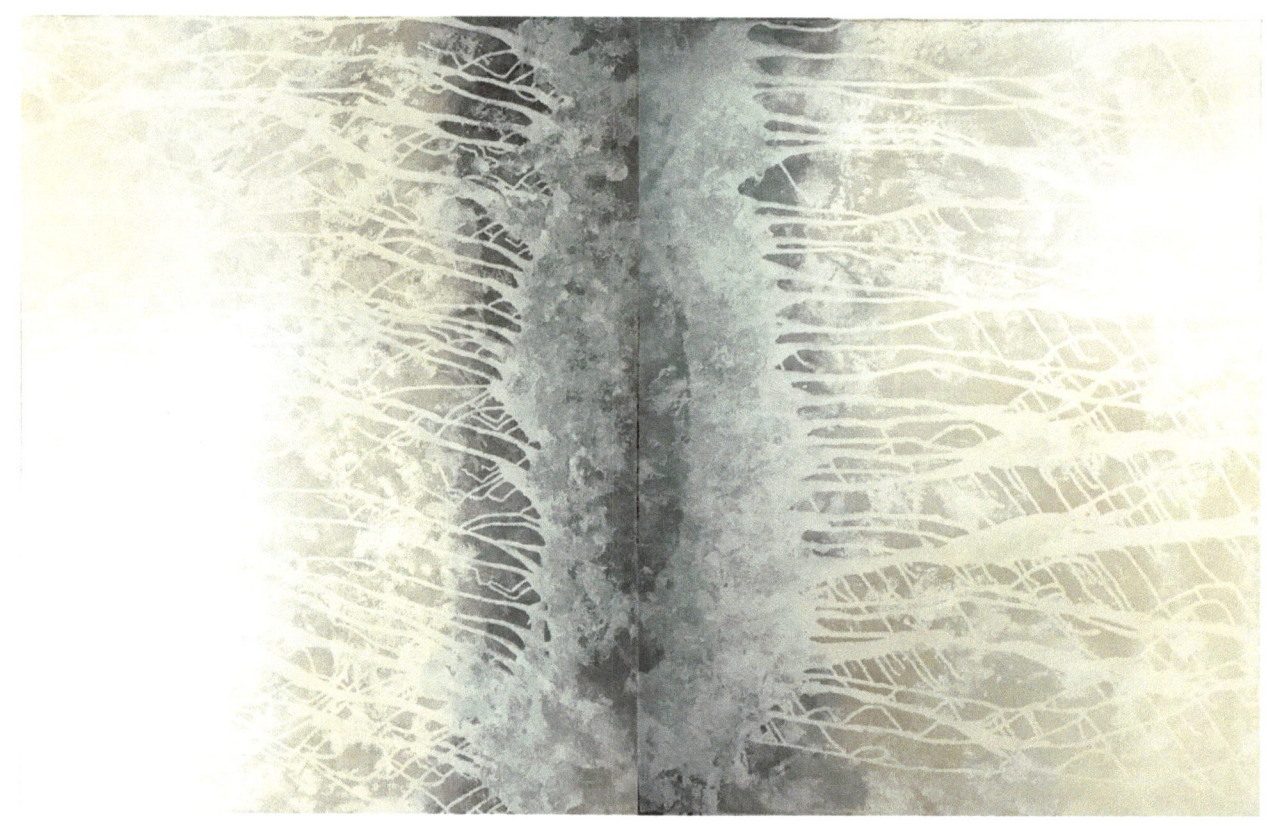

White Water Light #1; 2018; 58"x88"; two pieces 58"x44" each; acrylic on canvas; (can be hung vertical or horizontal)

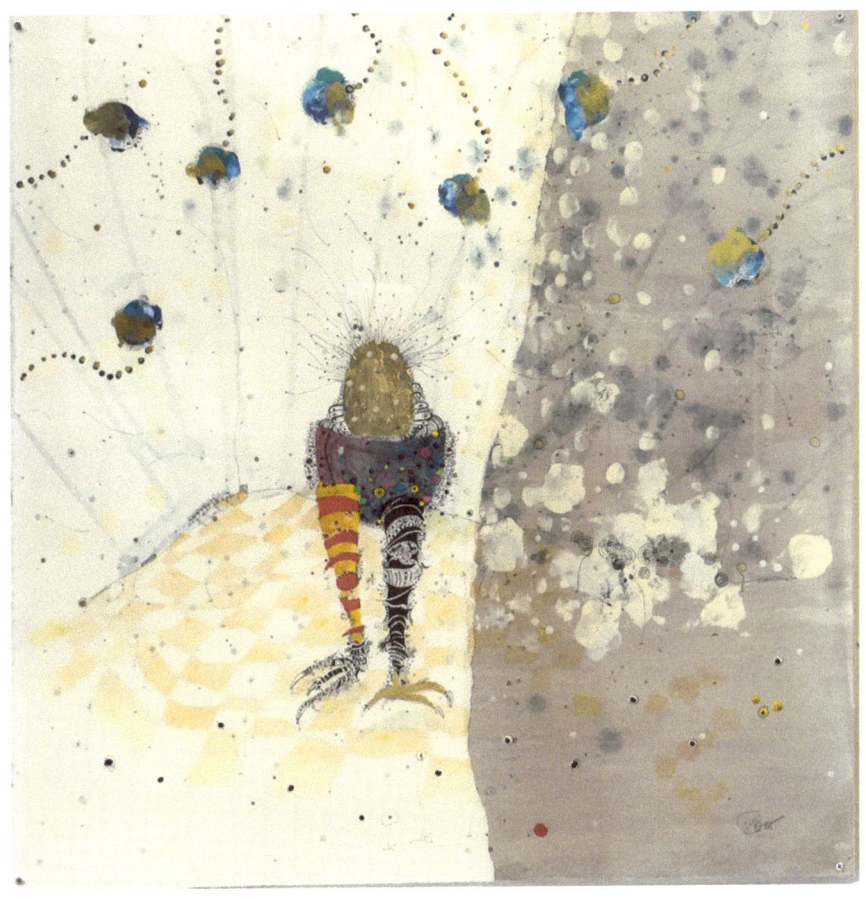

The Egg Walking: 2015; 24"x24"; mixed media on panel

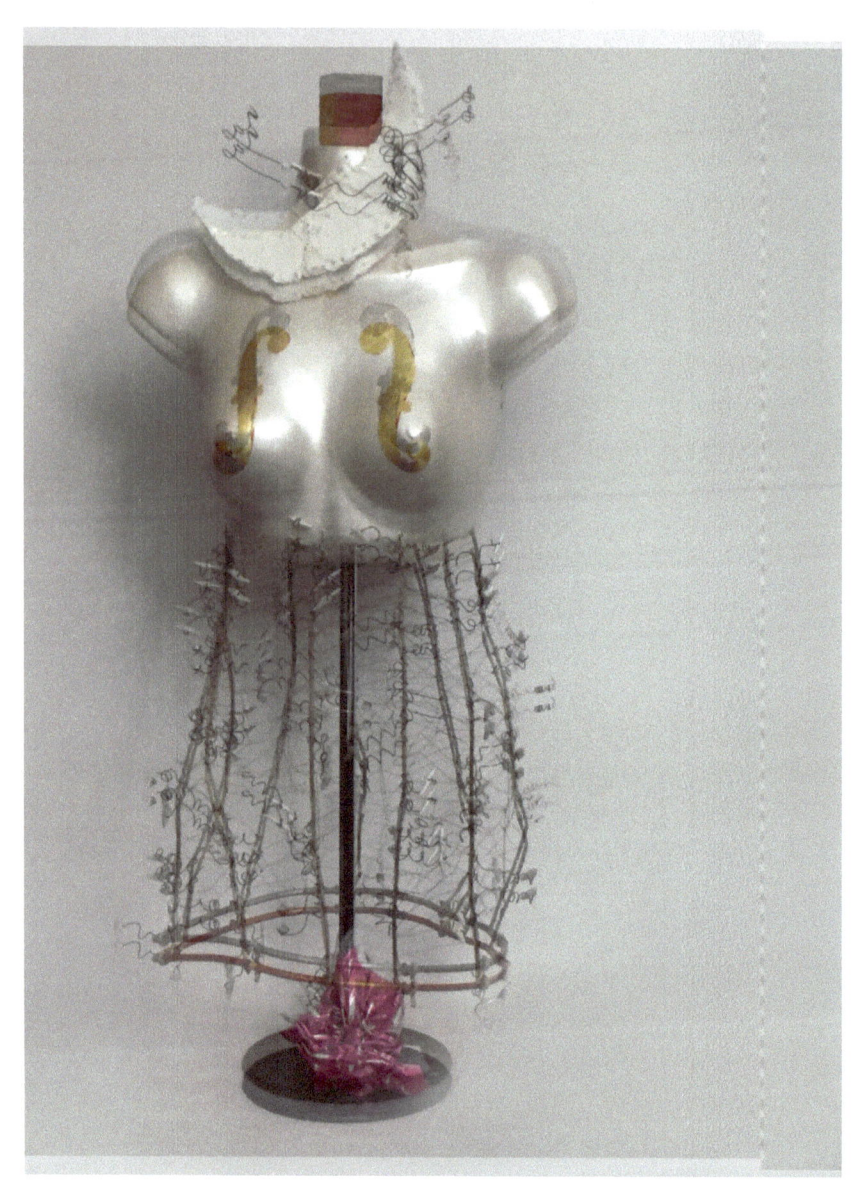

We Danced; 2016; approx; 36"x15"; mixed media

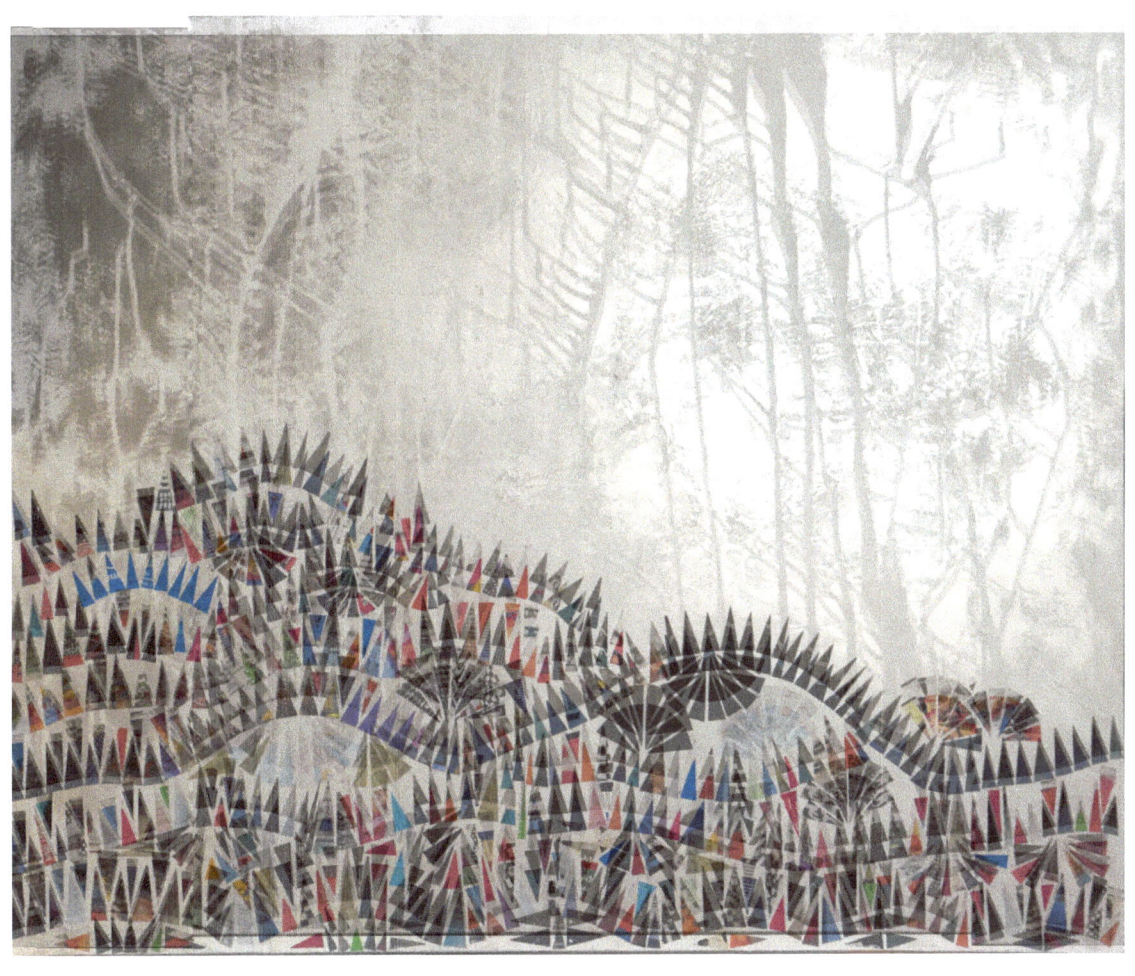

Festival of Fans; 2018; 48"x60"; acrylic, collage on canvas

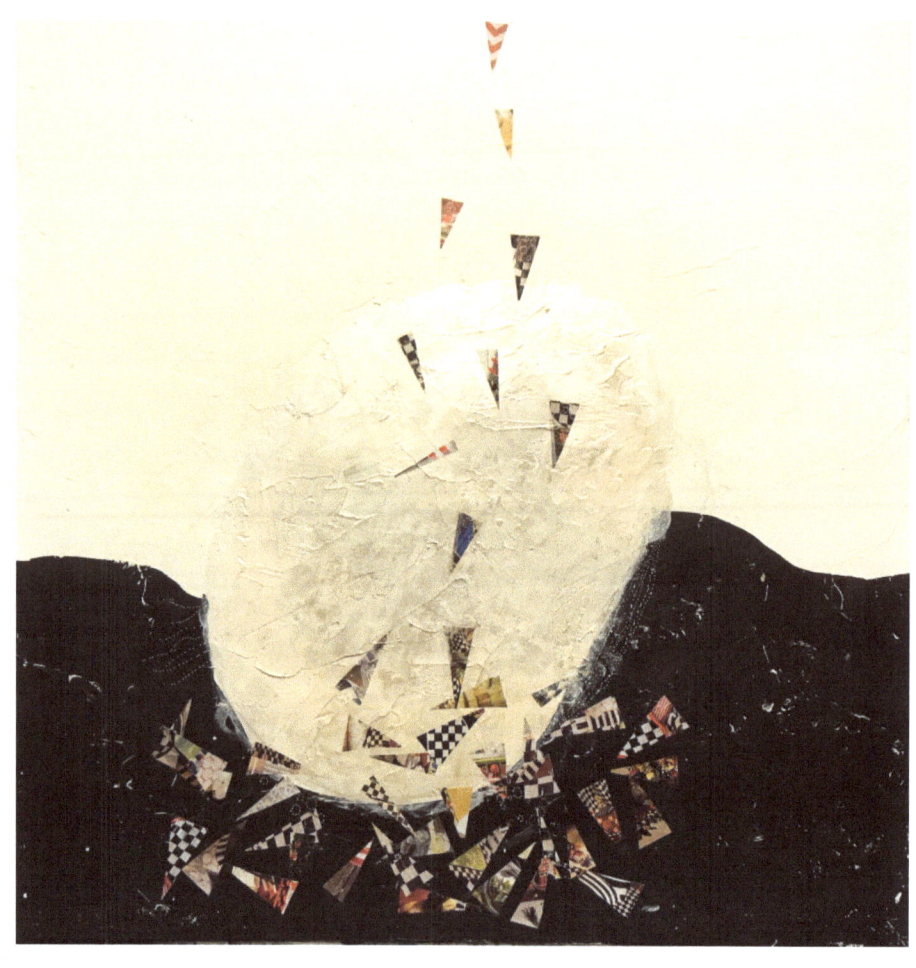

Passing Through; 2019; 30"x30"; mixed media on canvas

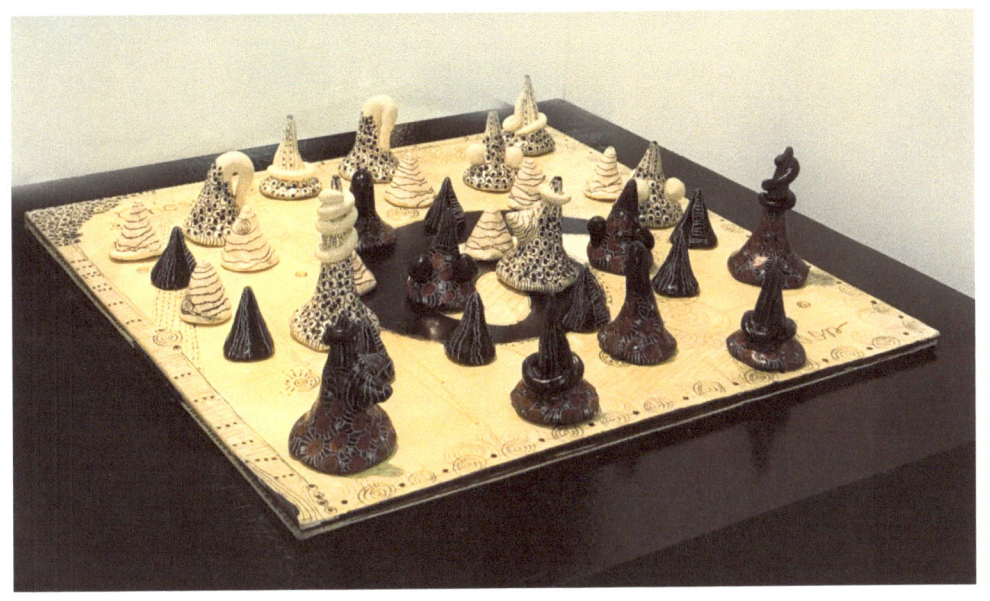

CHESS Set, Spiral Series; 2012; hand shaped polymer clay, and drawn upon folded double record album for chess board. It opens to be played on.

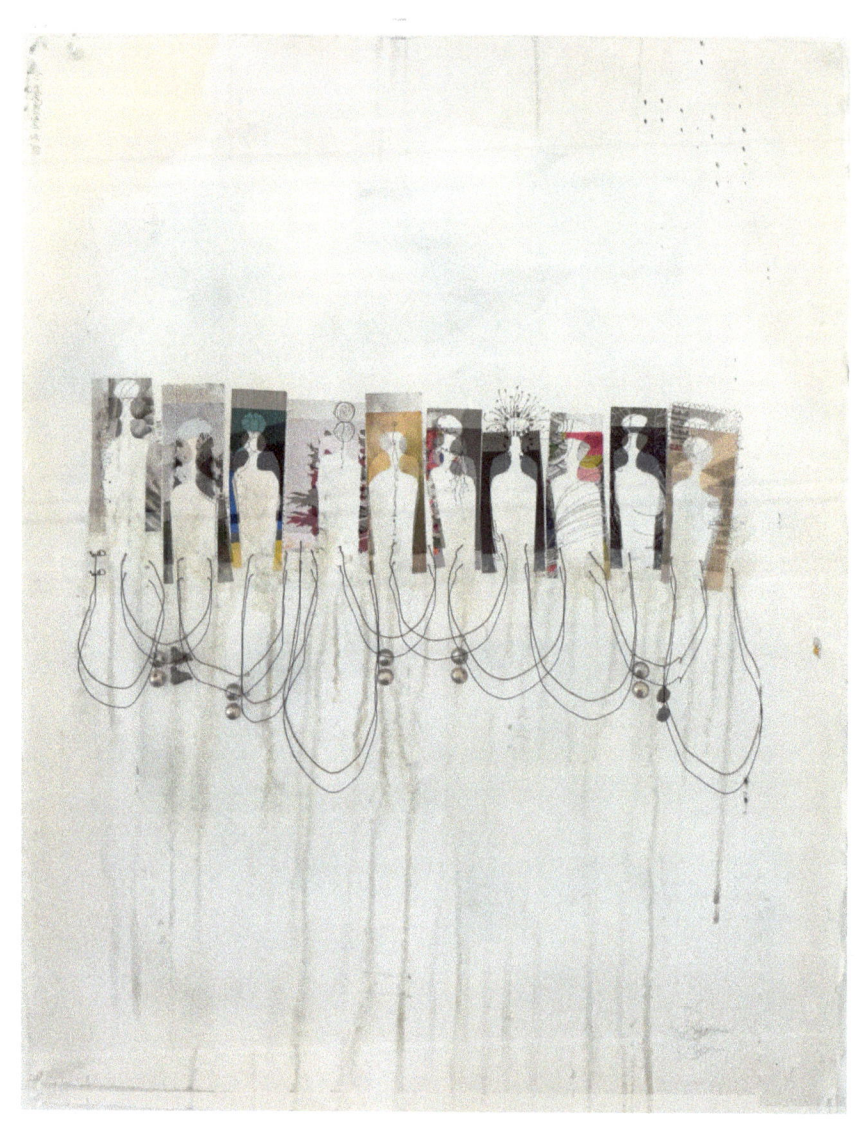

The Magic of Ten; 2017; 30"x22"; mixed media on paper

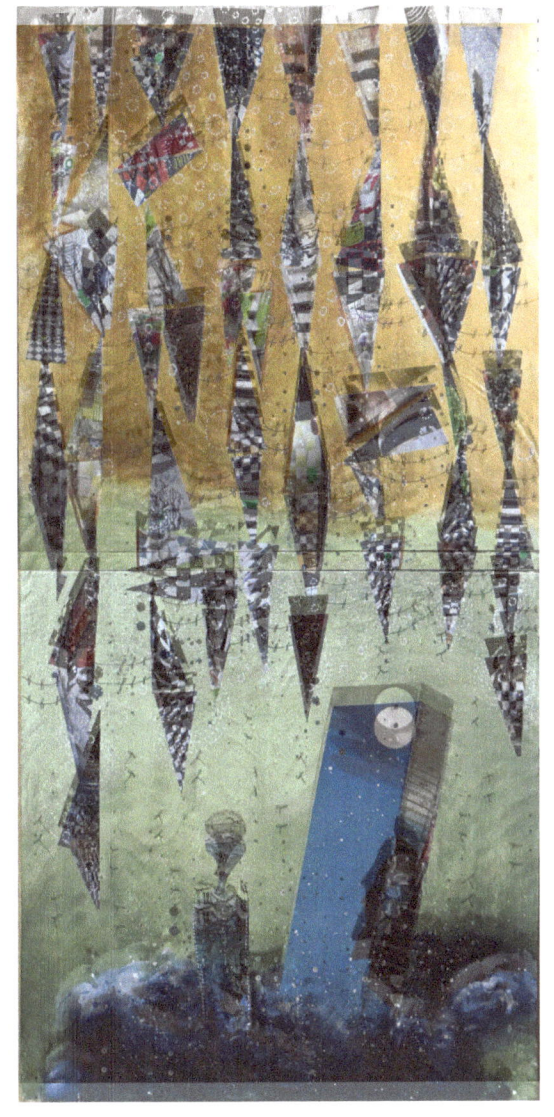

The Unseen Monolith; 2019; 24"x12"; mixed media on panel

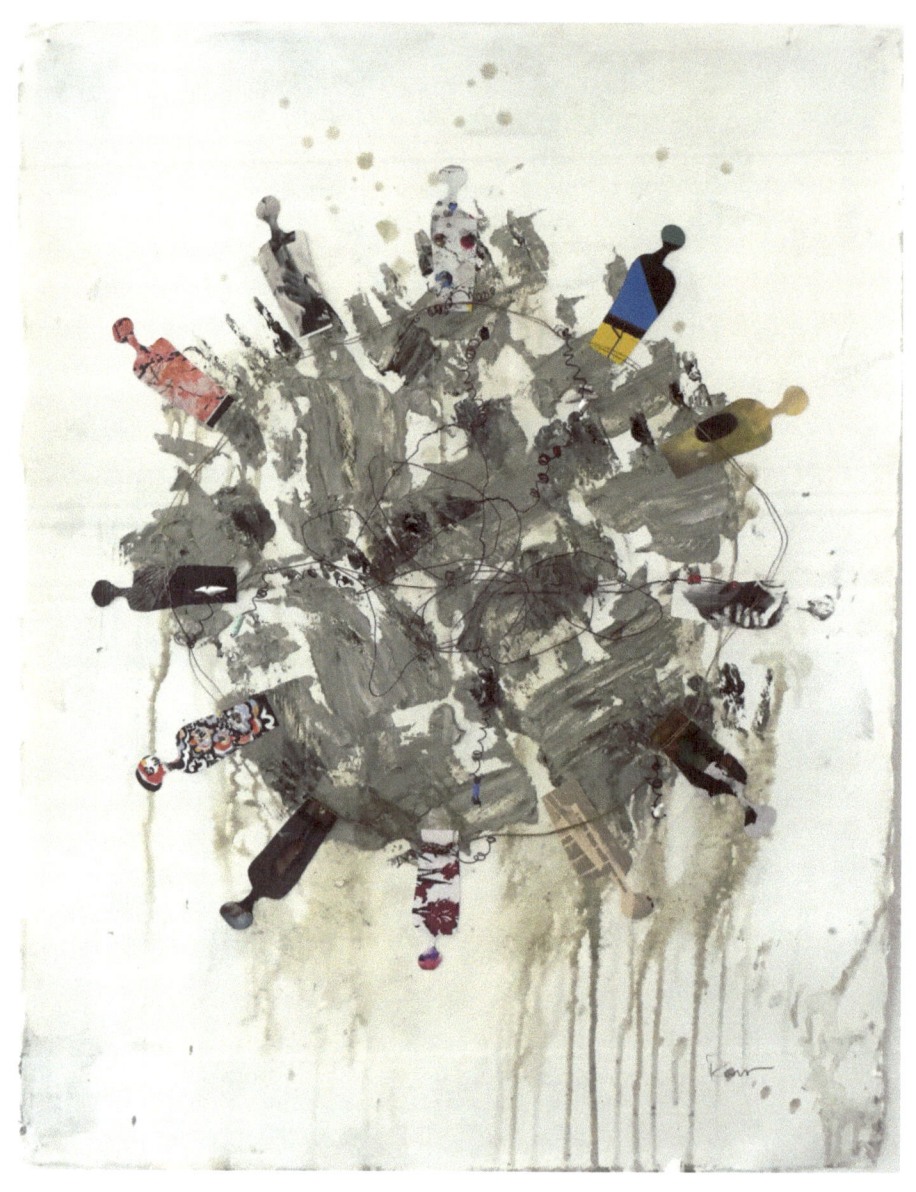

The ONE Circle; 2017; 30"x22"; mixed media on paper

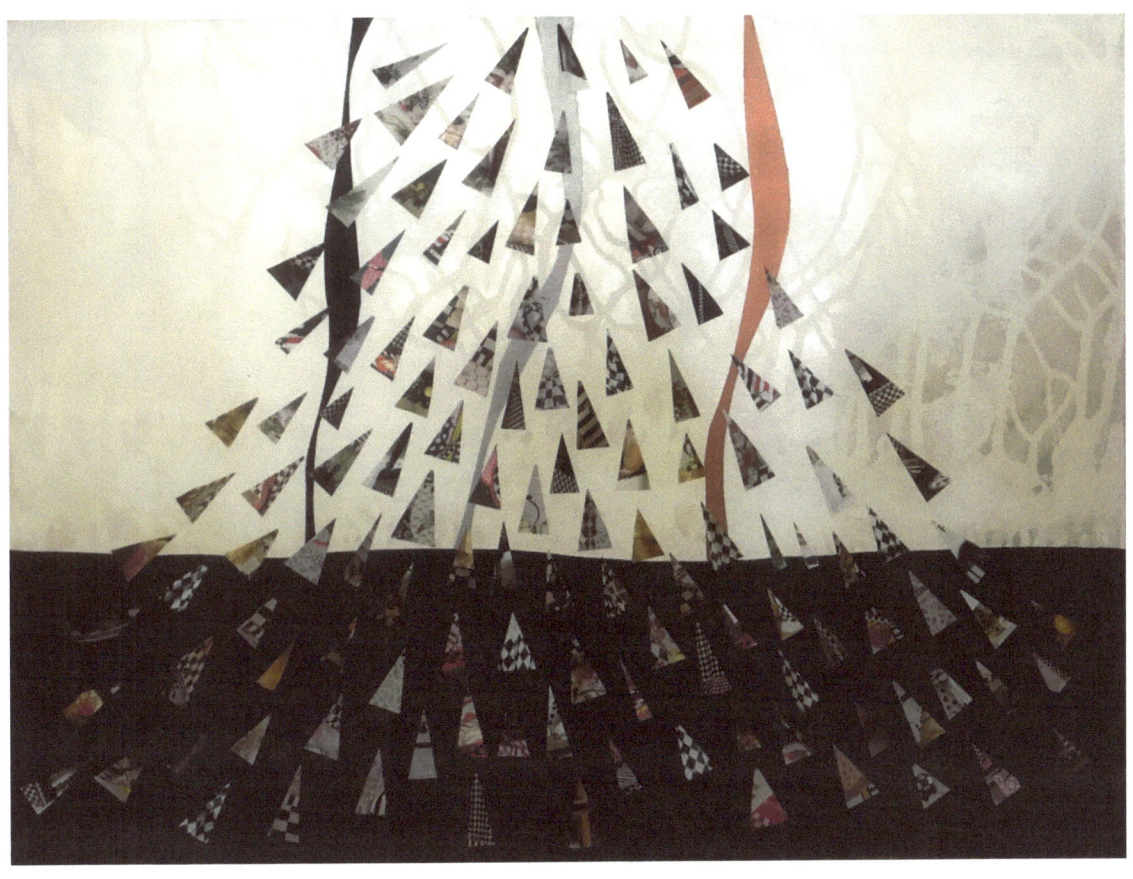

That's The Way…; 2019; 30"x40"; acrylic, collage on canvas;
(can be hung vertical or horizontal)

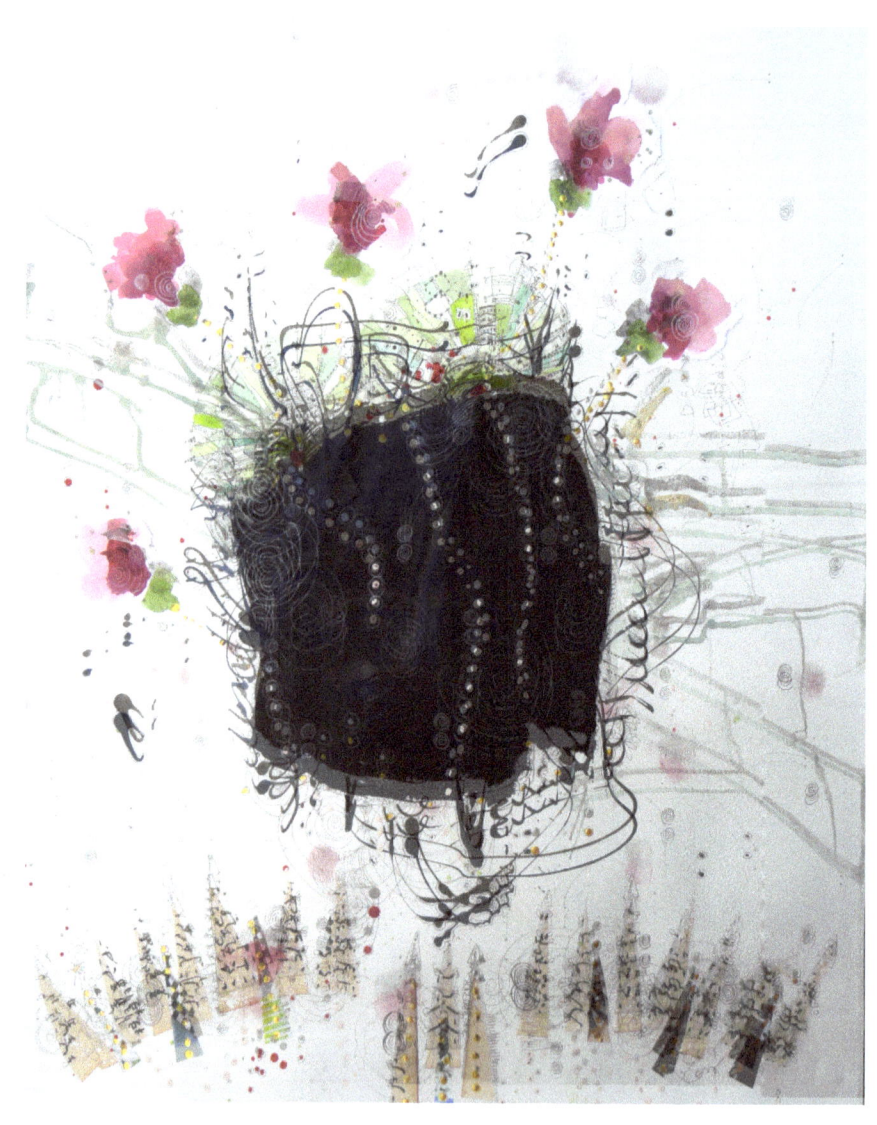

Dances with Flowers; 2016; 30"x22"; mixed media on paper

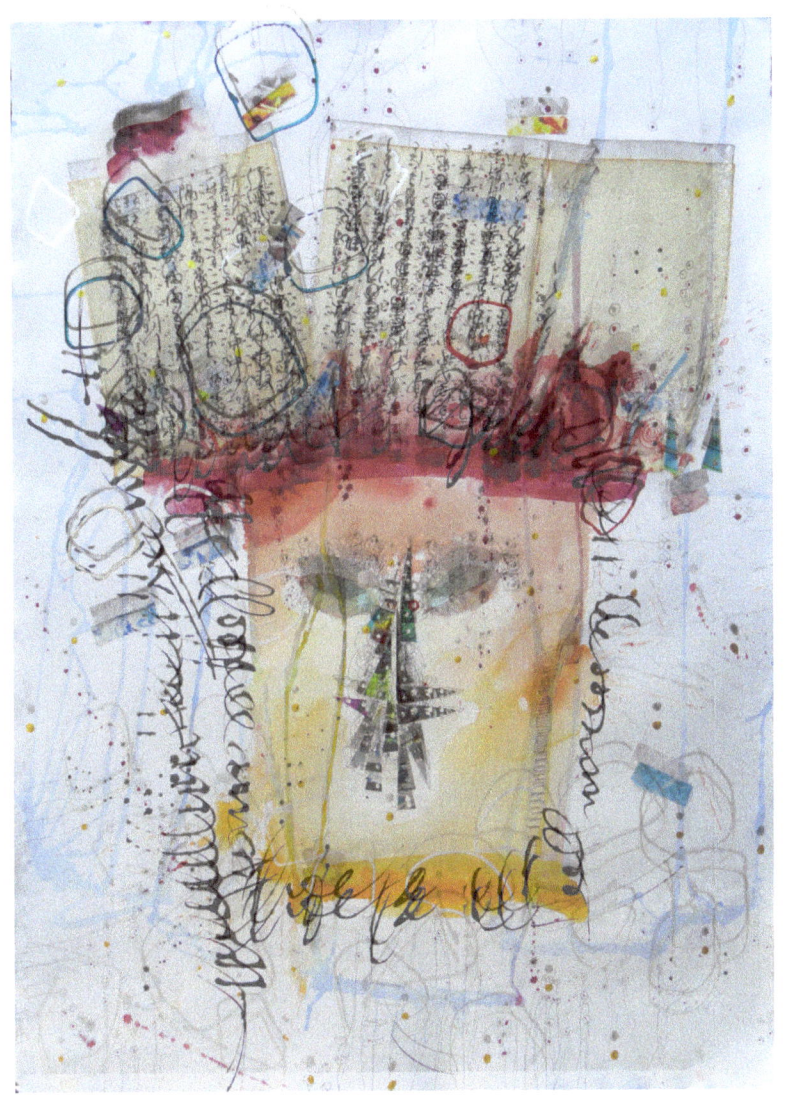

Face It!; 2016; 30"x22"; mixed media on paper

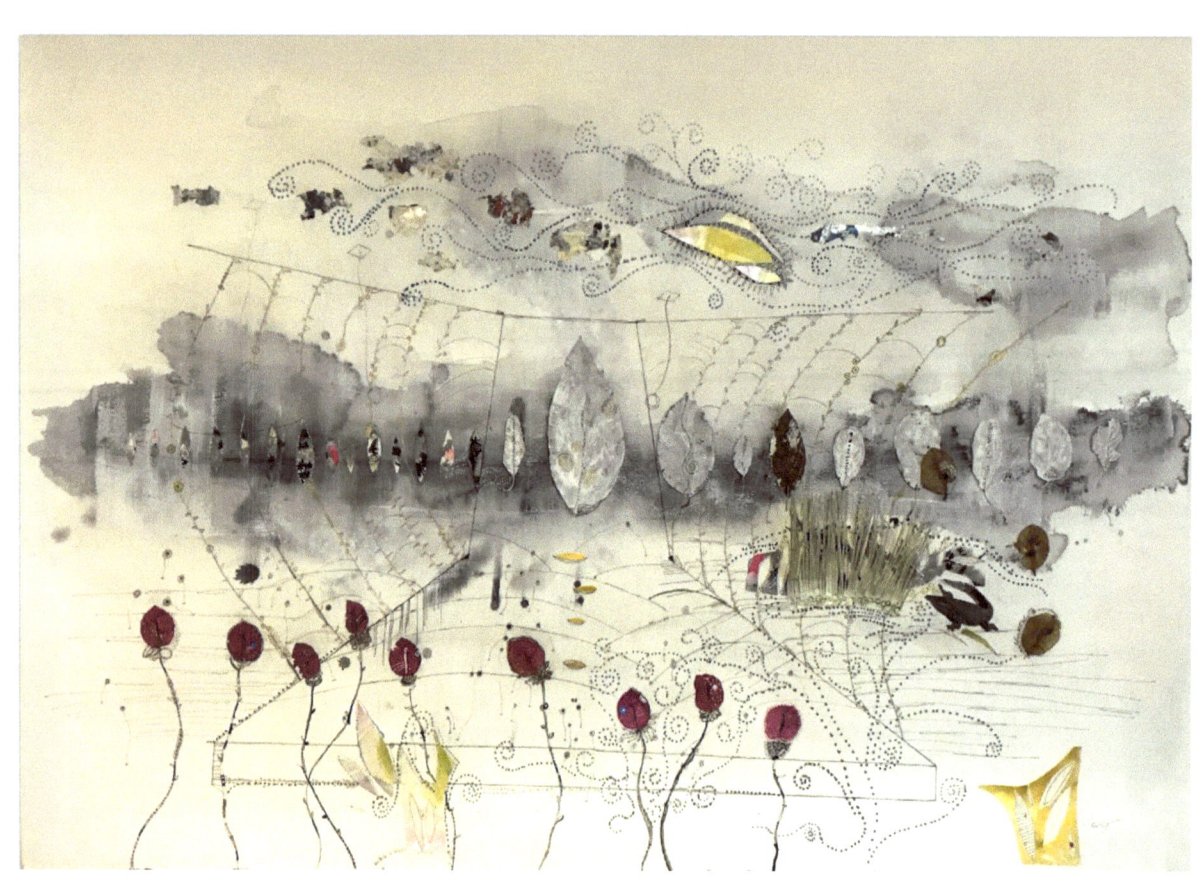

And as We Wind On Down the Road; 2018; 32"x44"; mixed media on paper

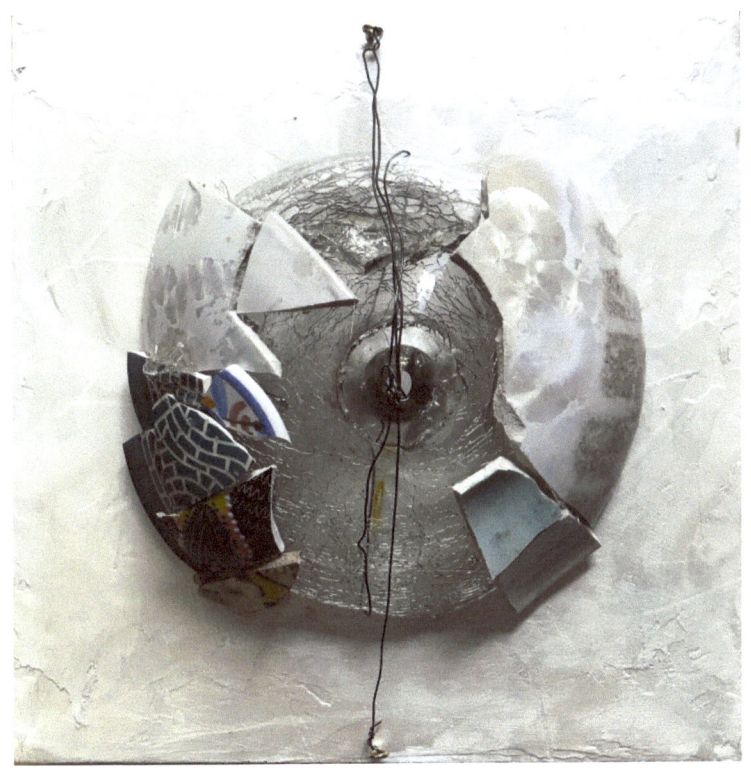

Simply Round; 2019; 10"x10" canvas

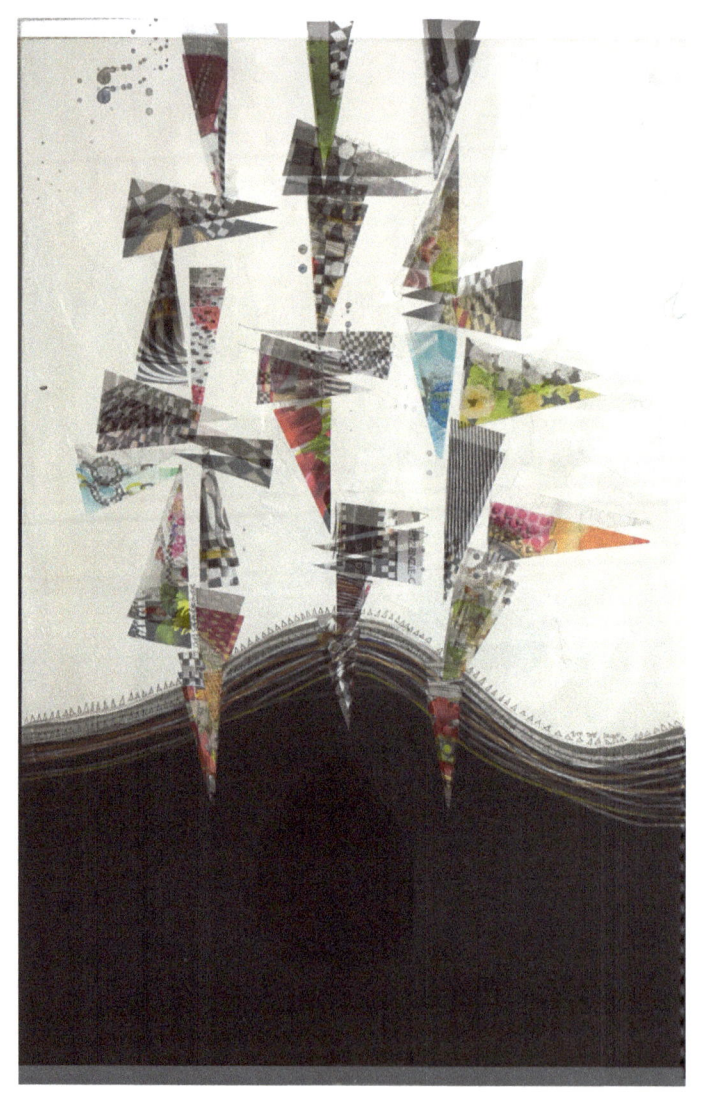

What Lays Benieth; 18"x12"; mixed media on panel

Karrie Ross :

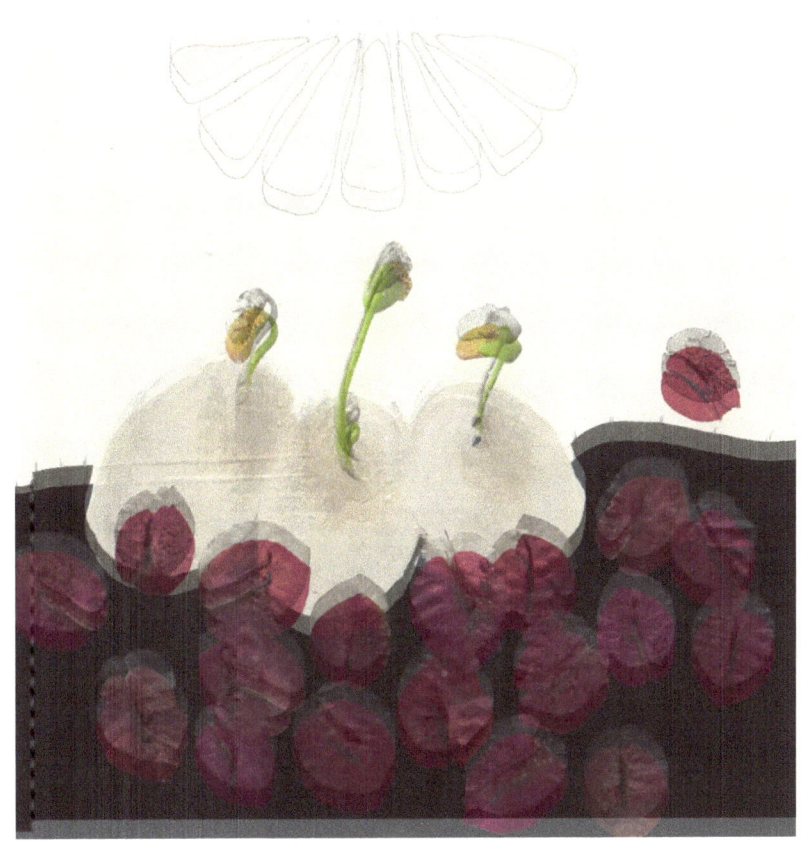

Bougainvilleggs; 2019; 12"x12"; mixed media on panel

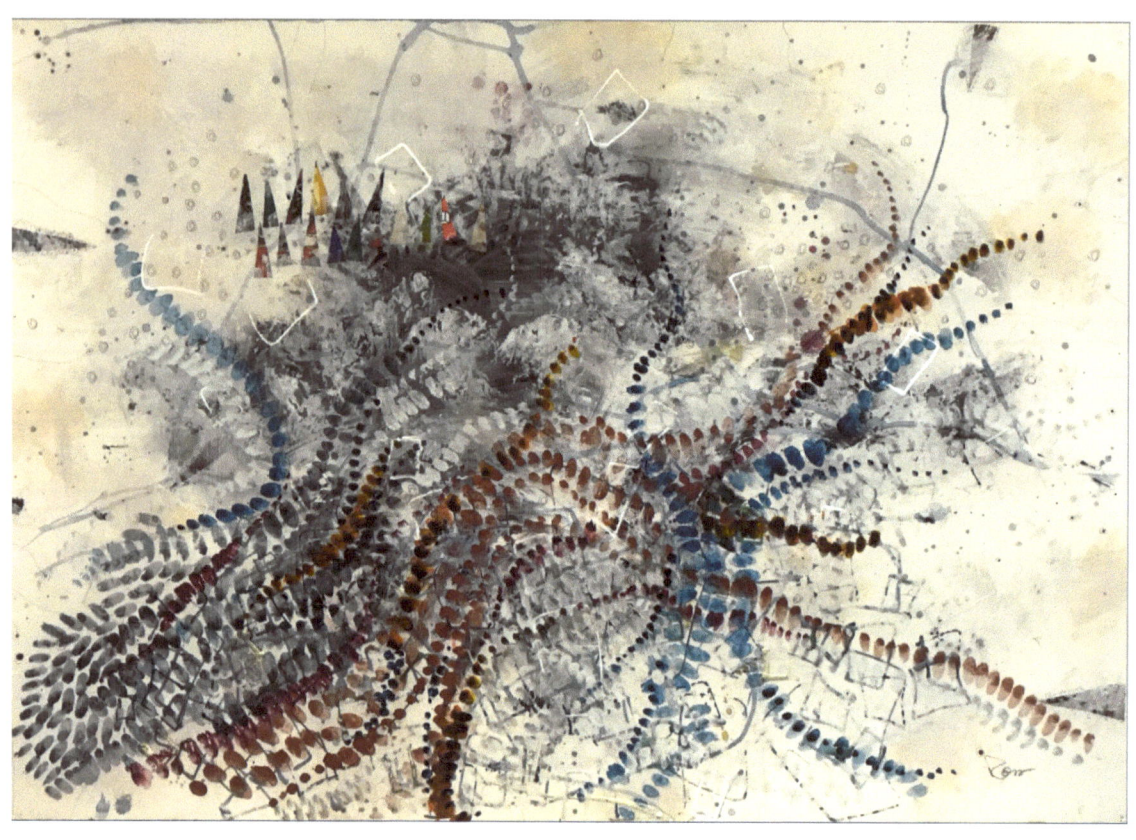

One is Never Lost When a Path Still Exists; 2018; 32"x44"; mixed media on paper

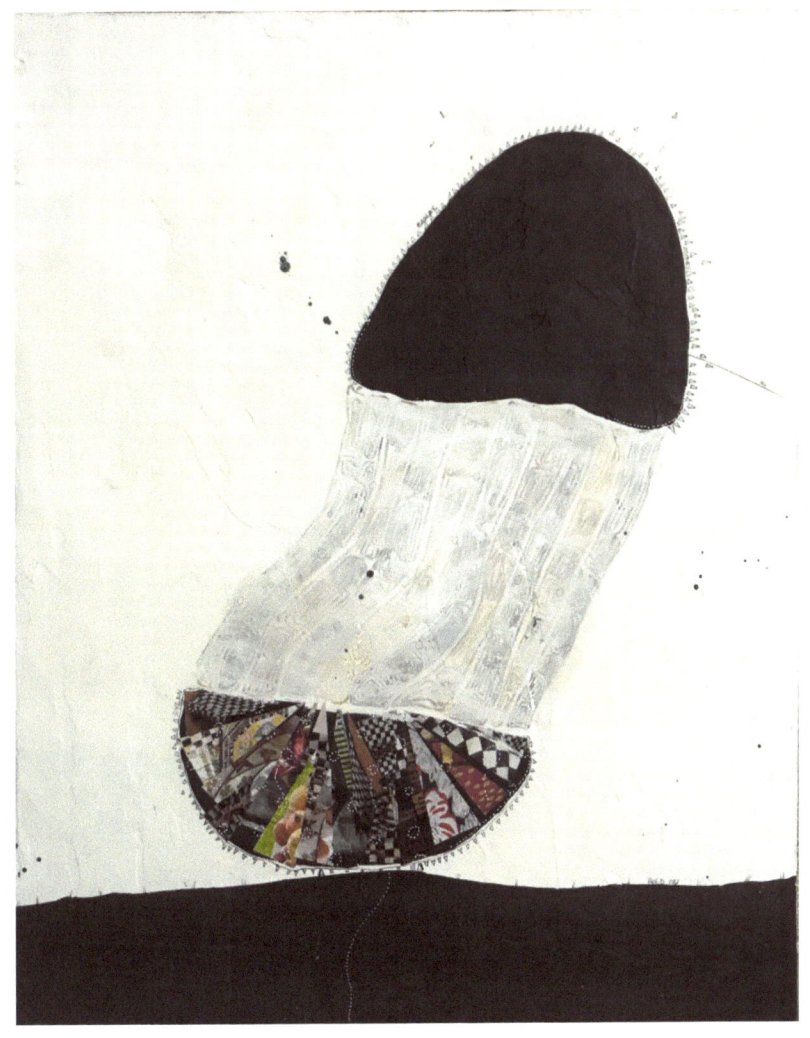

The Egg Inside; 2019; 20"x16"; acrylic, collage, ink on canvas

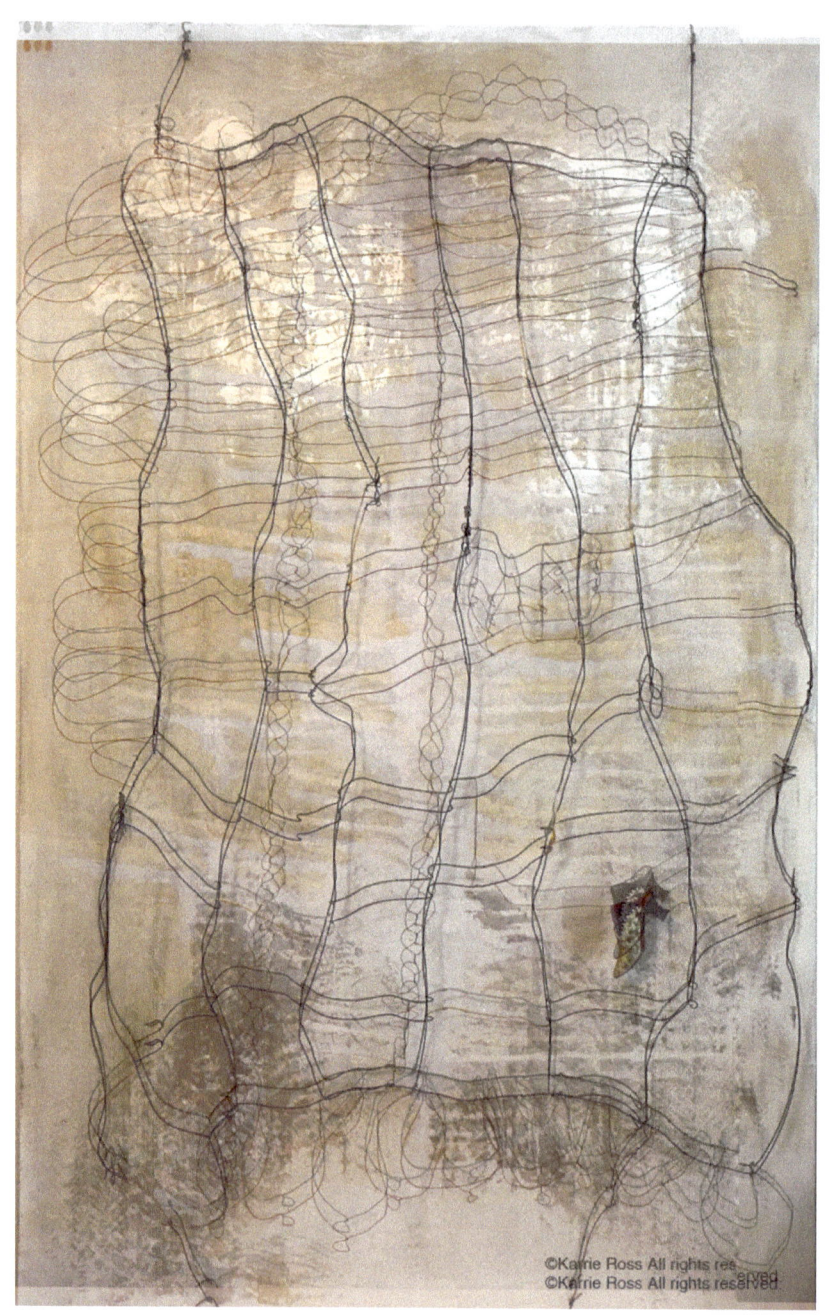

Climbing; 2018; 58"x36"; mixed media on canvas

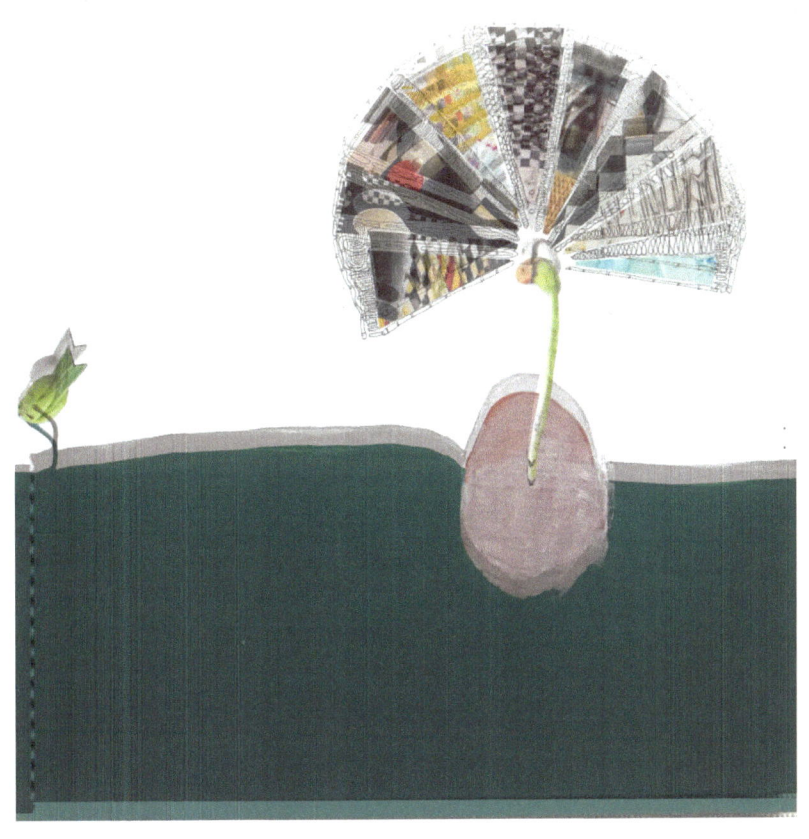

Sprouting Egg; 2019; 12"x12"; mixed media on panel

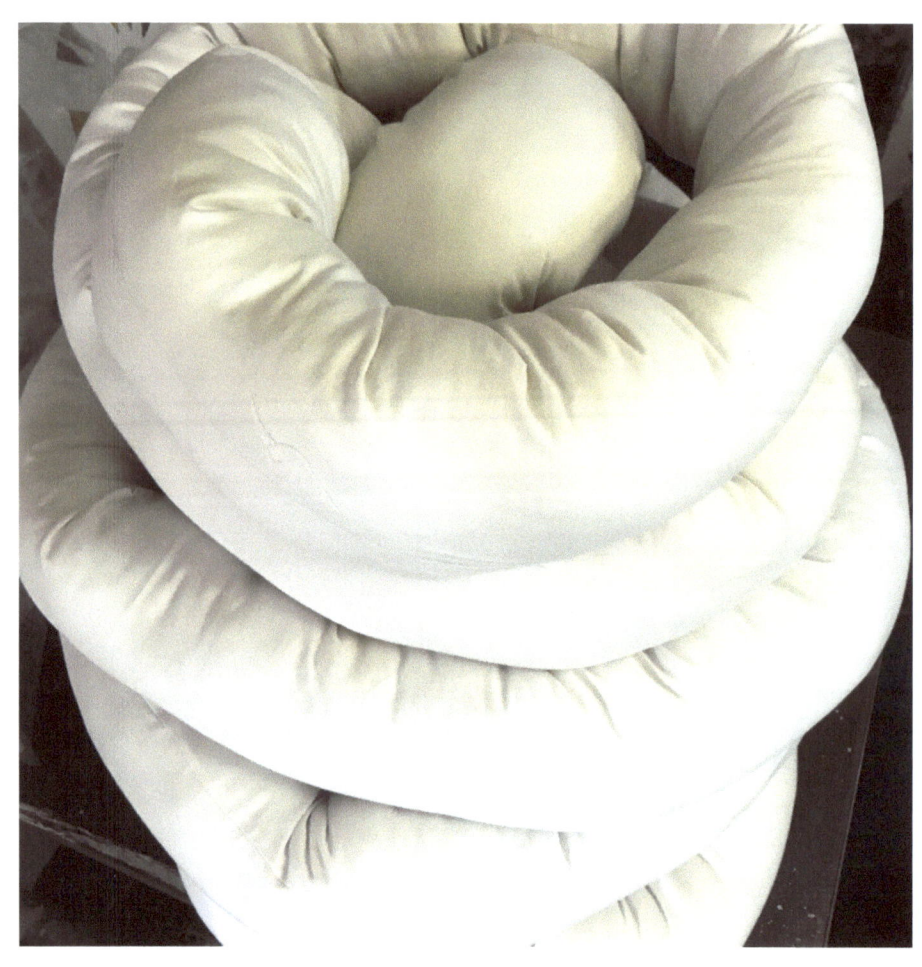

Egg Rolled; 2019; 5" x 30'; stuffed fabric and molded into shapes

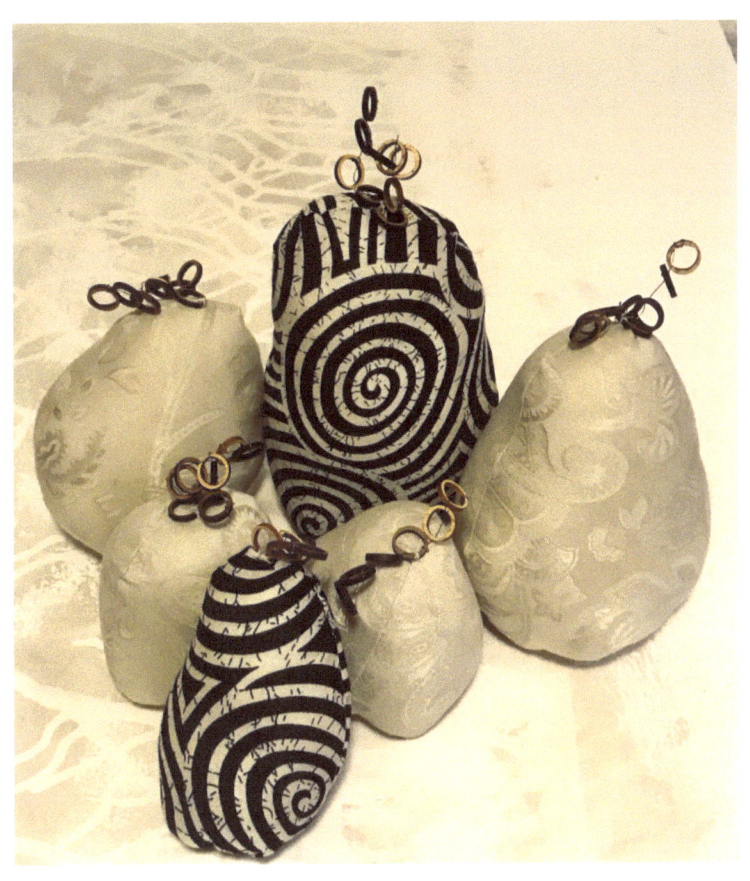

Lost Eggs; 2019; size varies from 3"x3" up to 7"x15"; recycled fabrics stuffed and painted on

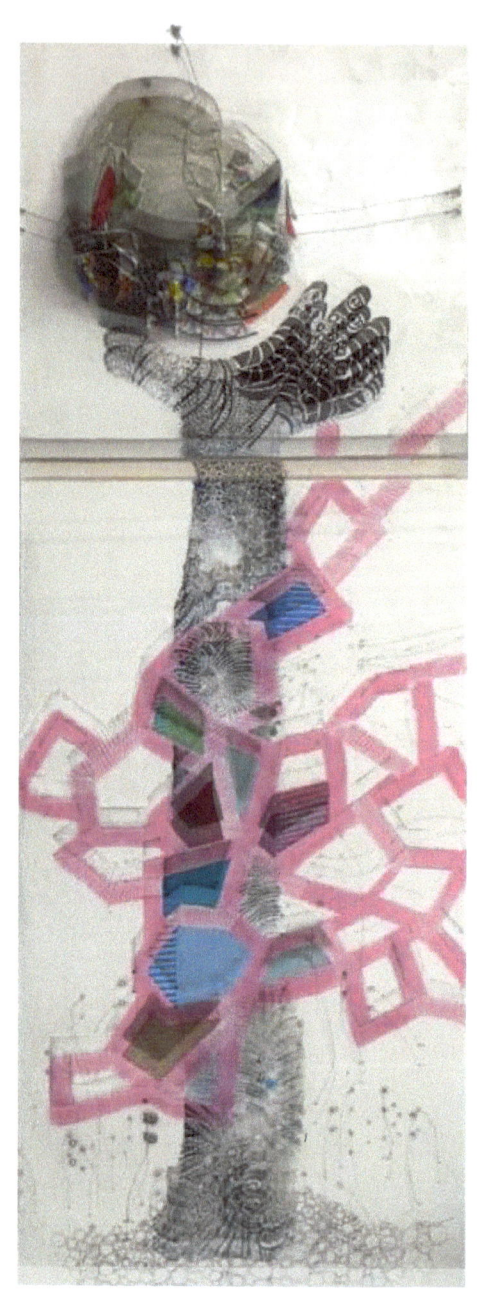

Catch; 2019; 36"x12"; mixed media on panel

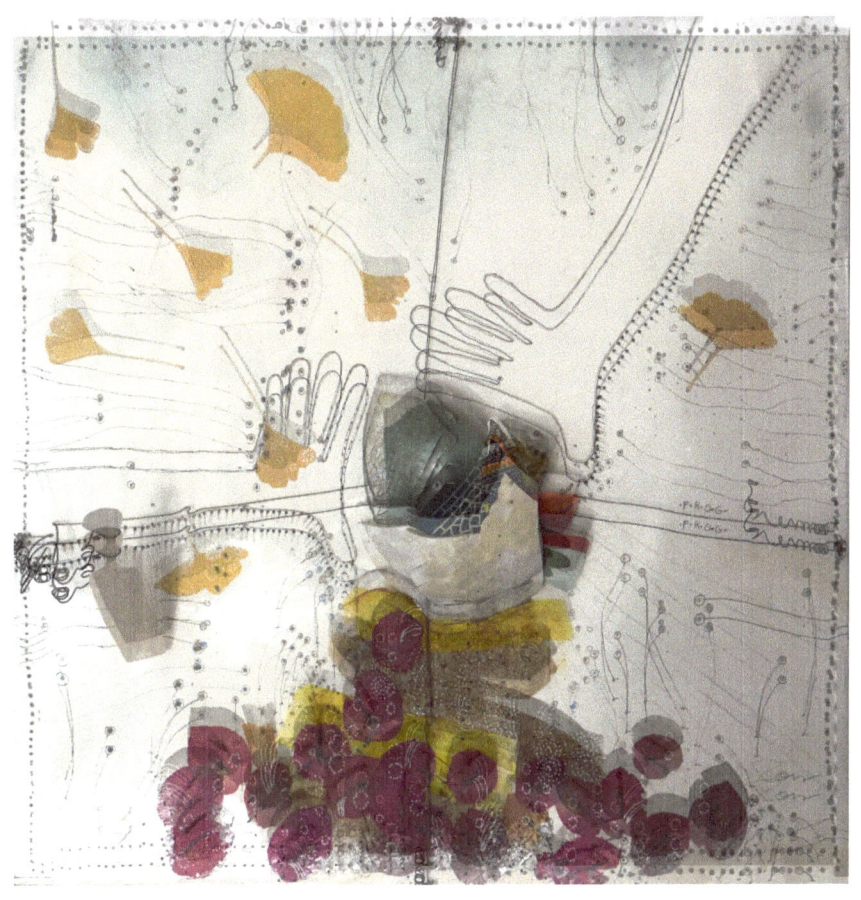

The Egg with Gingko Tea; 2019; 20"x20"; mixed media on panel

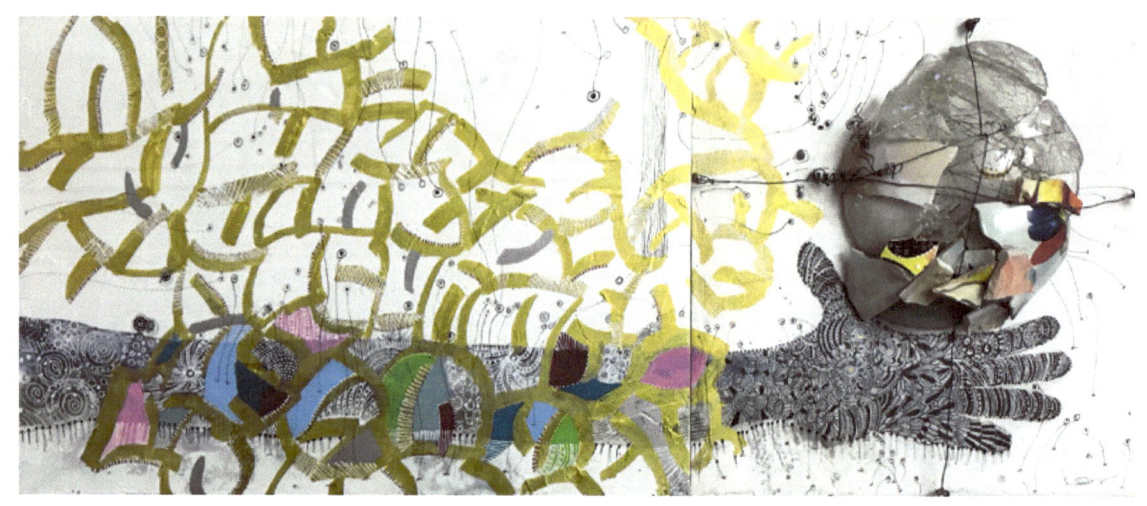

The Egg of the Golden Veil; 2019; 12"x30"; mixed media on panel

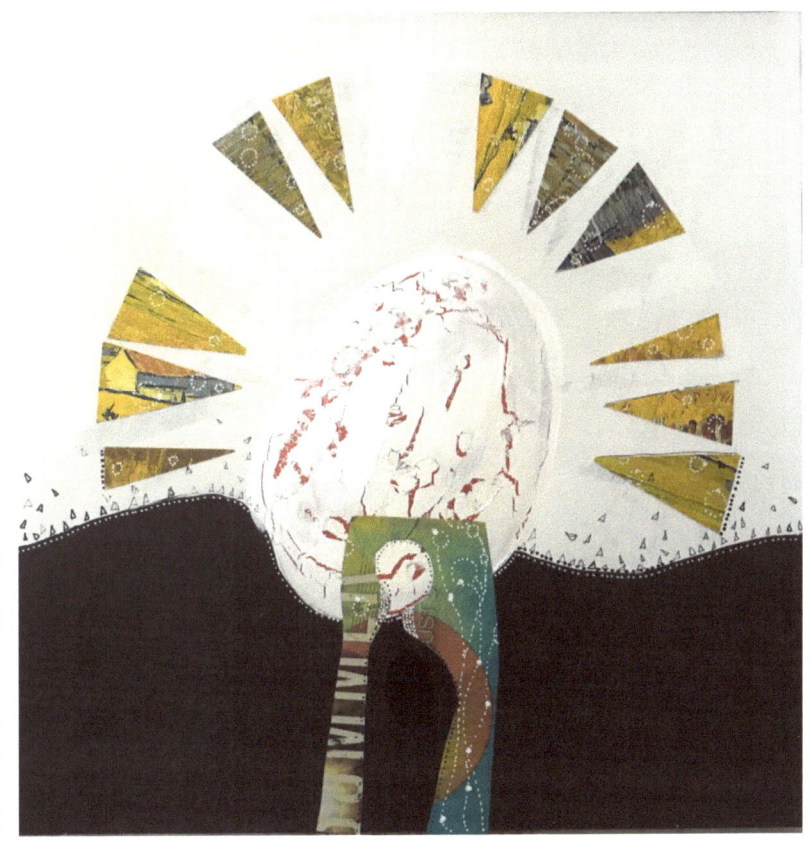

Wondering Why the Right Words Never Come; 2019; 12"x12"; mixed media on panel

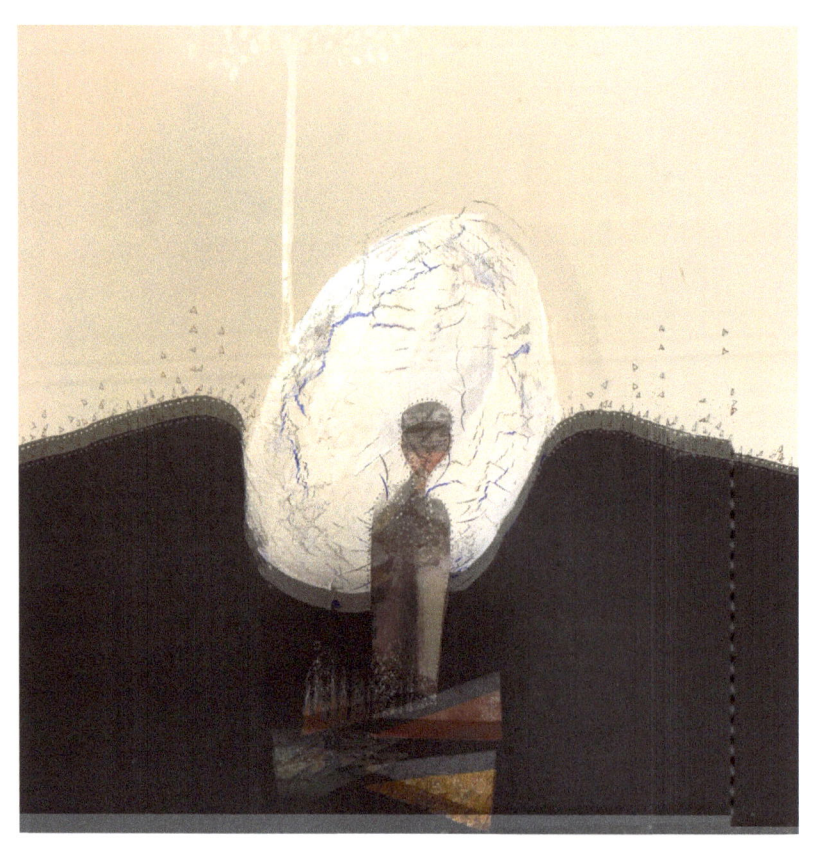

That's a Hard One!; 2019; 12"x12"; mixed media on panel

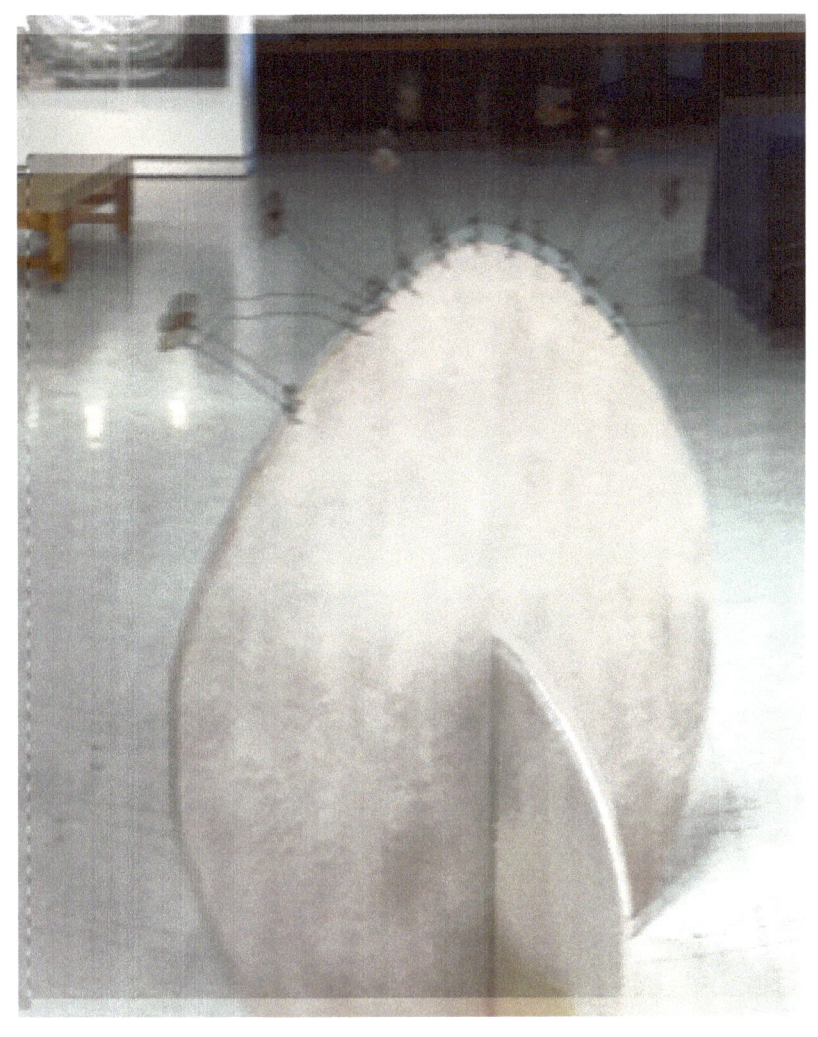

The EGG!; 2019; 48"x40"; mixed media on wood, handmade beads with wire

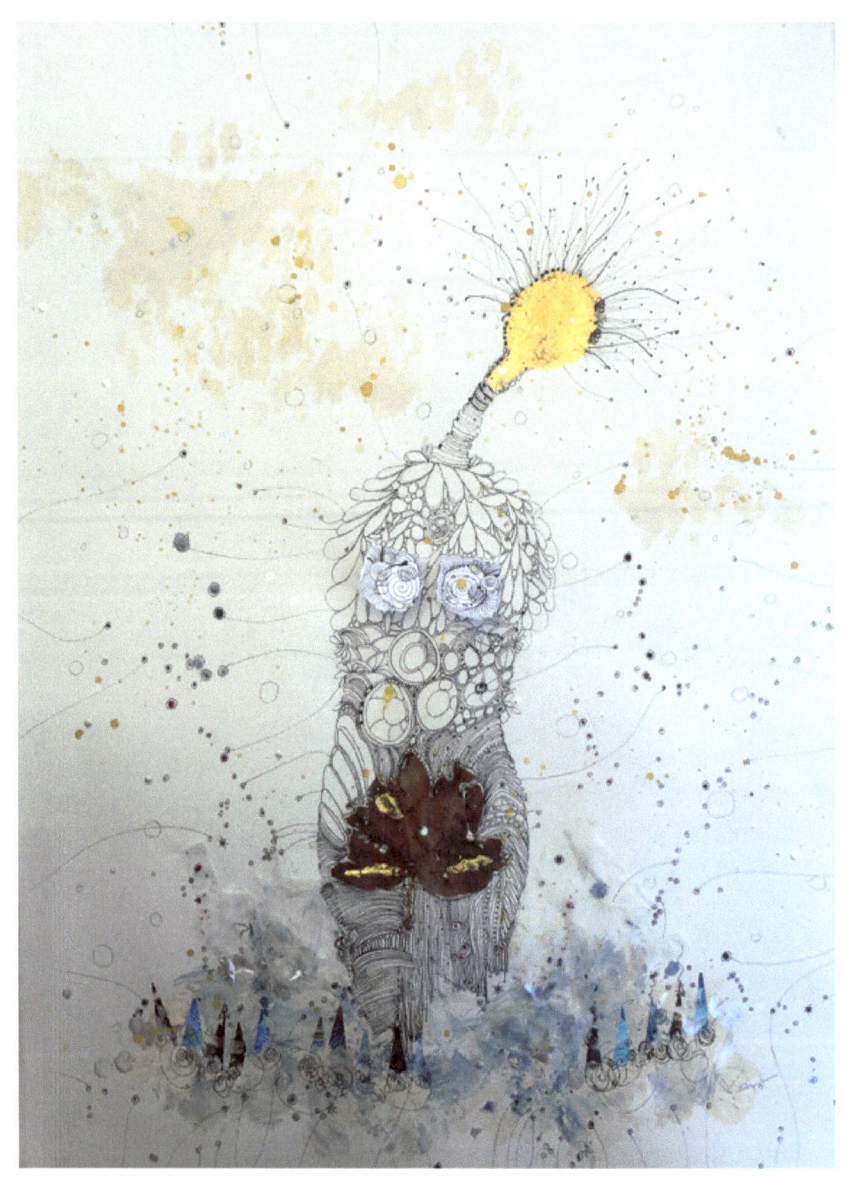

The ONE With Water; 2016; 30"x22"; mixed media on paper

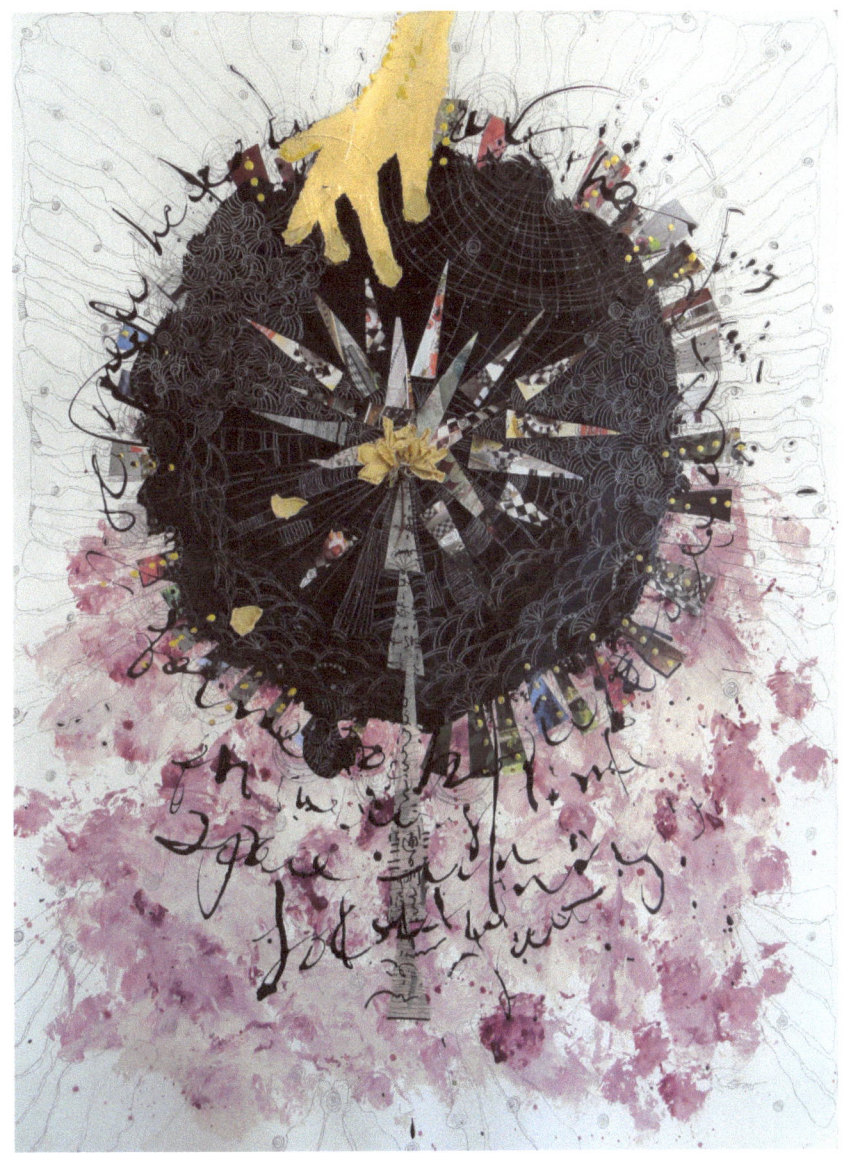

The Spark Within; 2016; 30"x22"; mixed media on paper

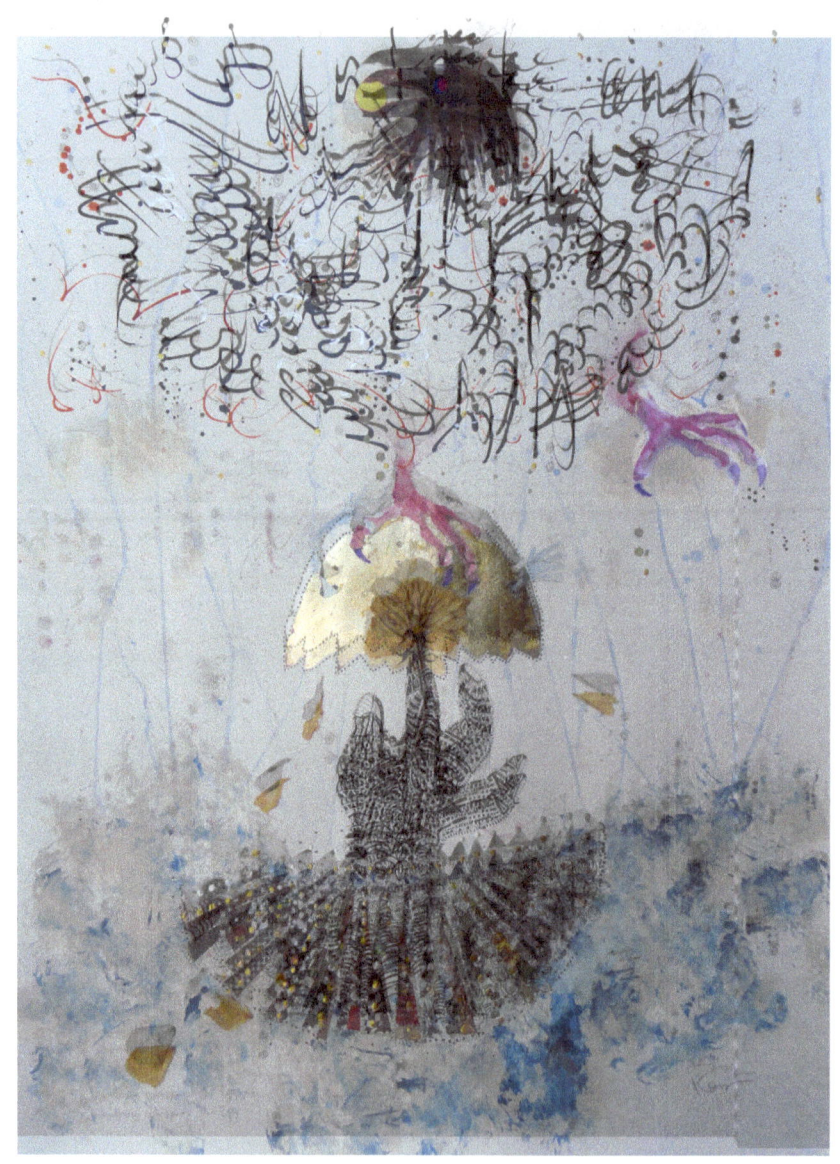

Cracked; 2016; 30"x22"; mixed media on paper

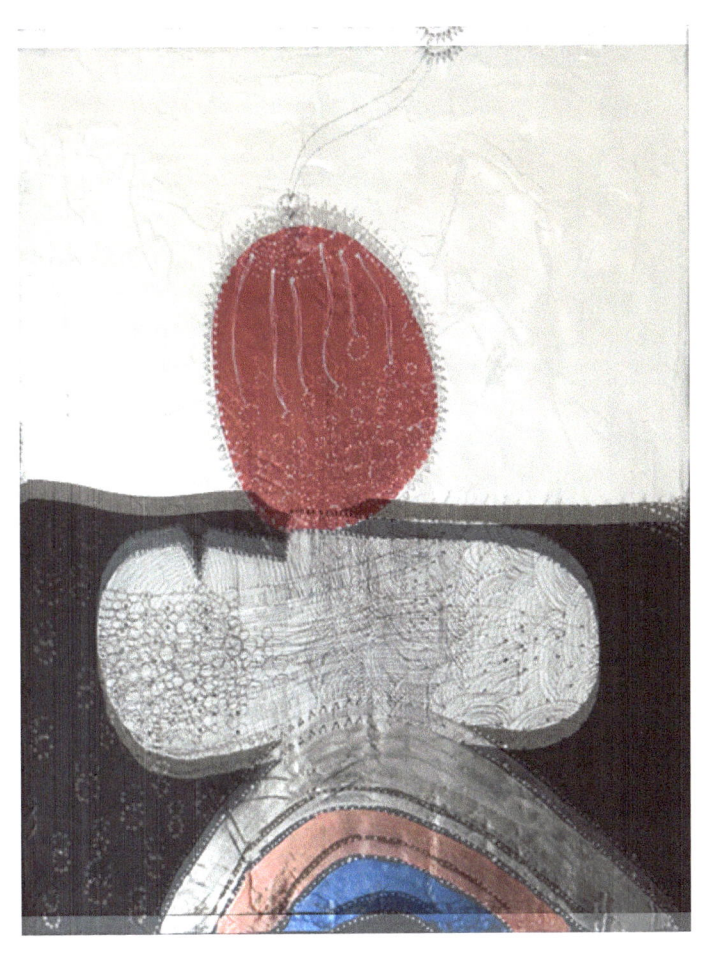

It's A Balancing Act; 2019' 14"x11"; acrylic, ink on canvas

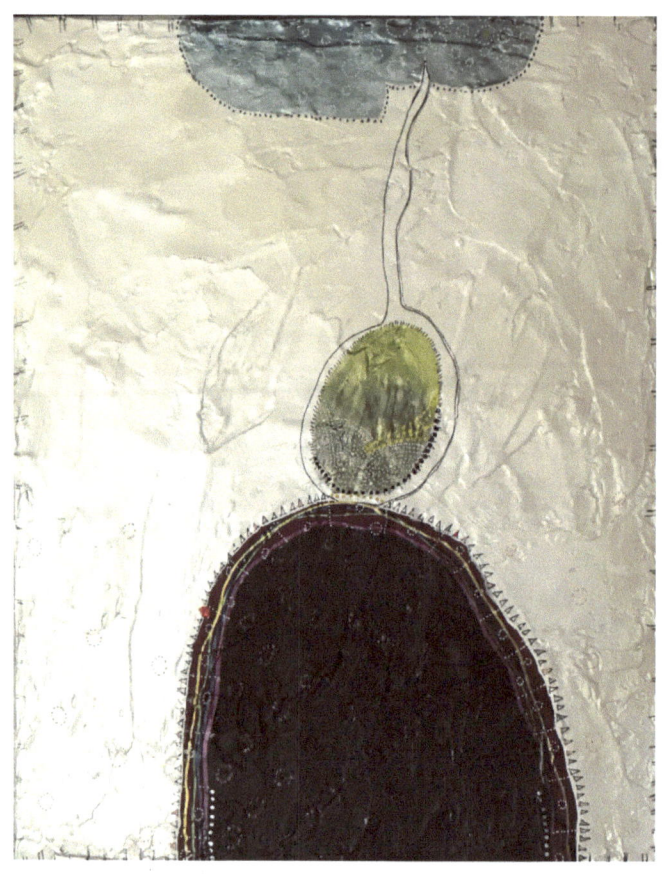

Love Will Keep Us Alive; 2019' 14"x11"; acrylic, ink on canvas

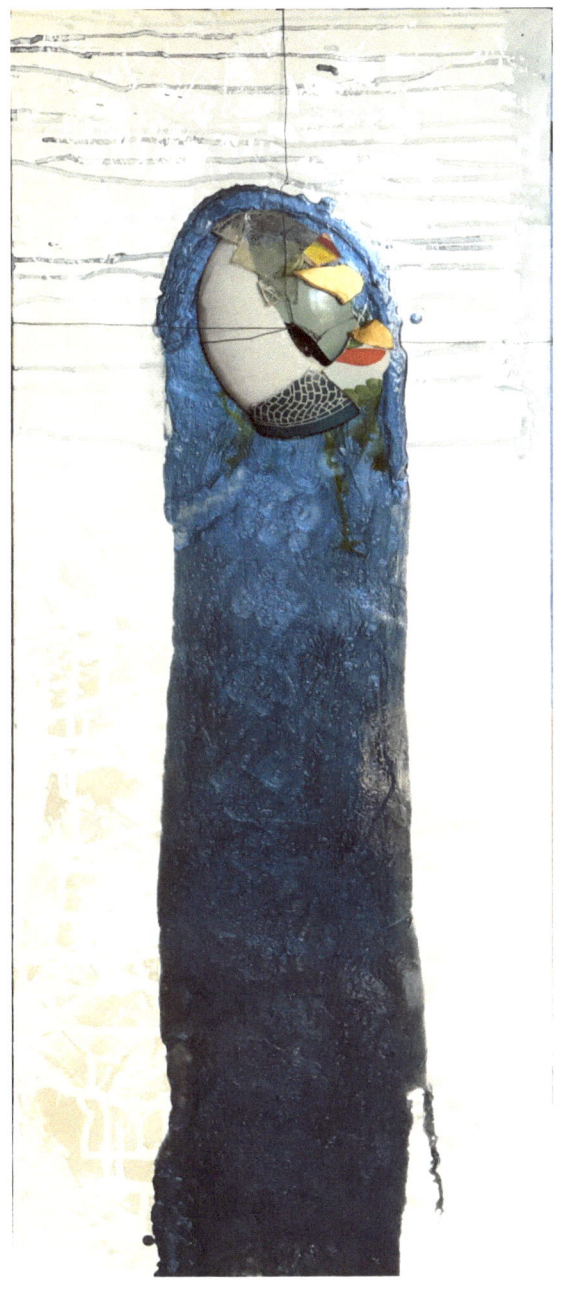

Climb the Highest Mountain; 2019; 36"x12"; acrylic on canvas

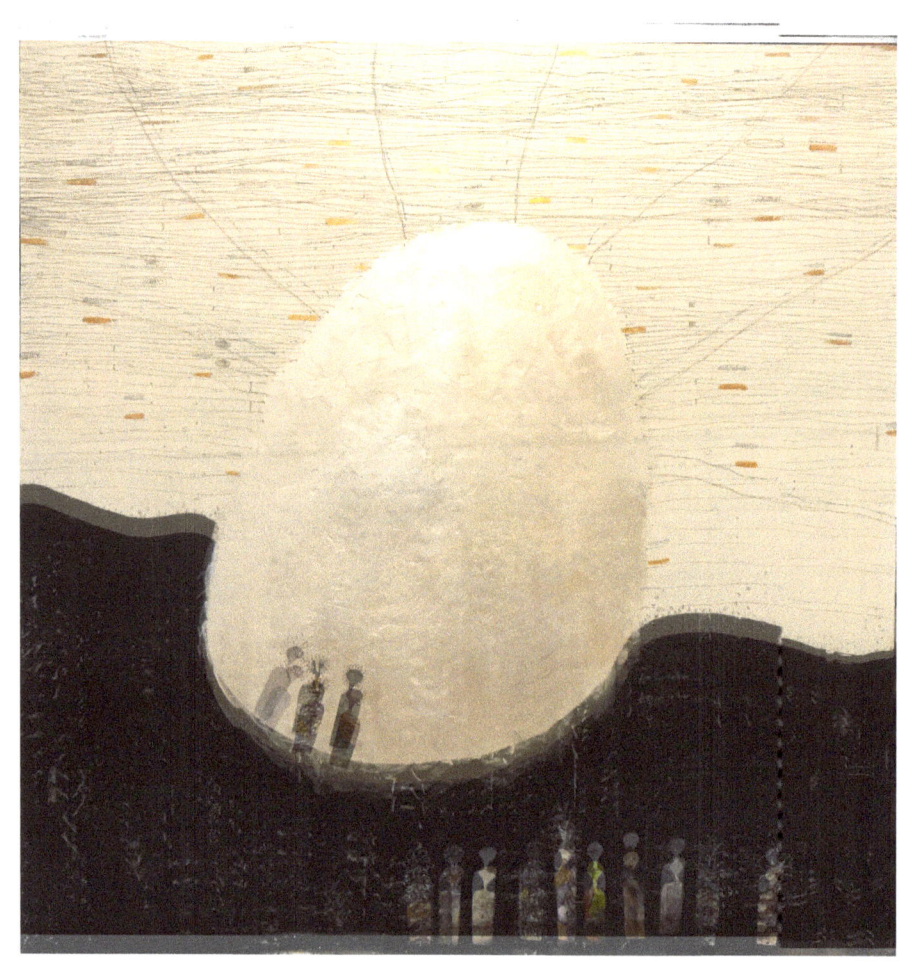

There are Moments of Pretend; 2019; 48"x48"; acrylic, collage on canvas

Karrie Ross :

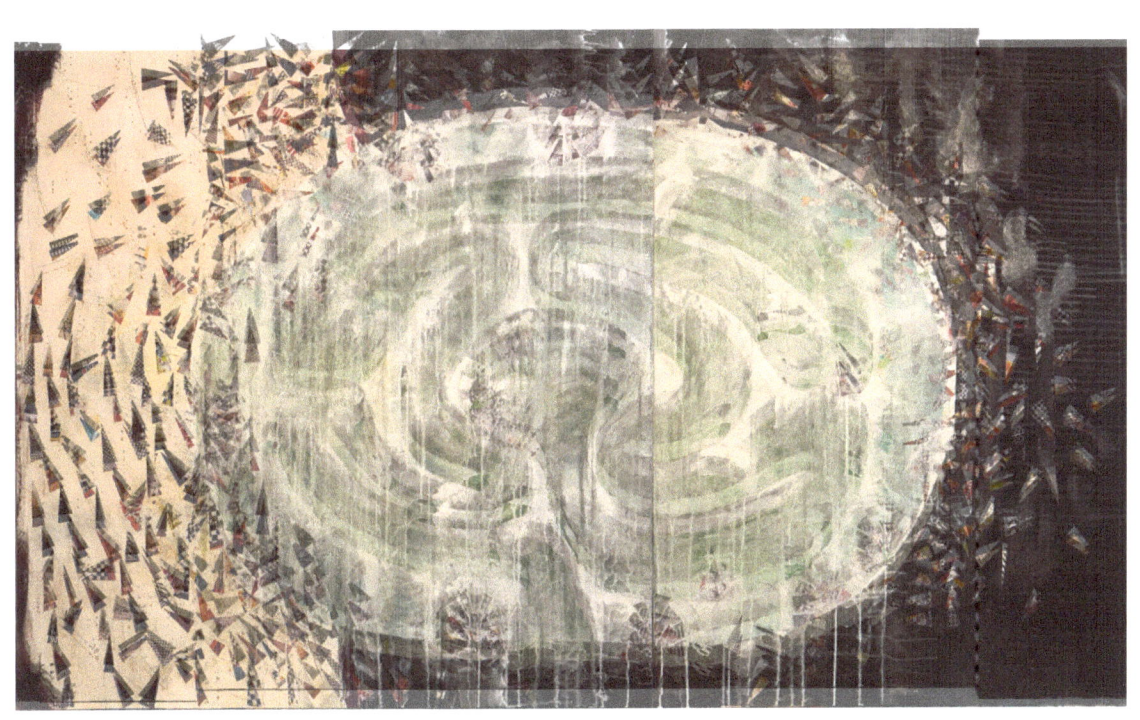

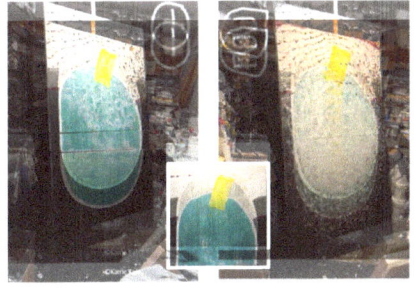
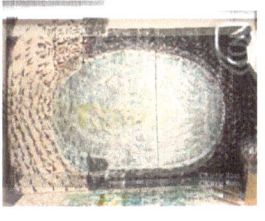

Cycle; 2019; 48"x84" /or/ 84"x48"; mixed media on canvas; (can hang either vertical or horizontal) Insert photo of process.

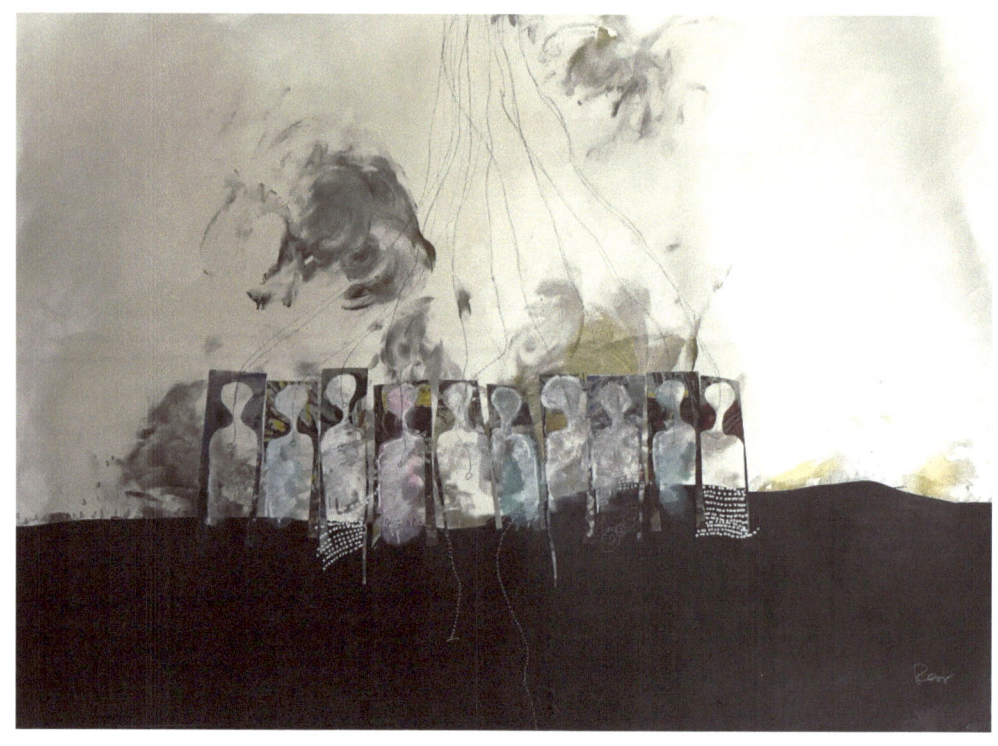

Holding the Line; 2019; 19"x28"; mixed media on paper

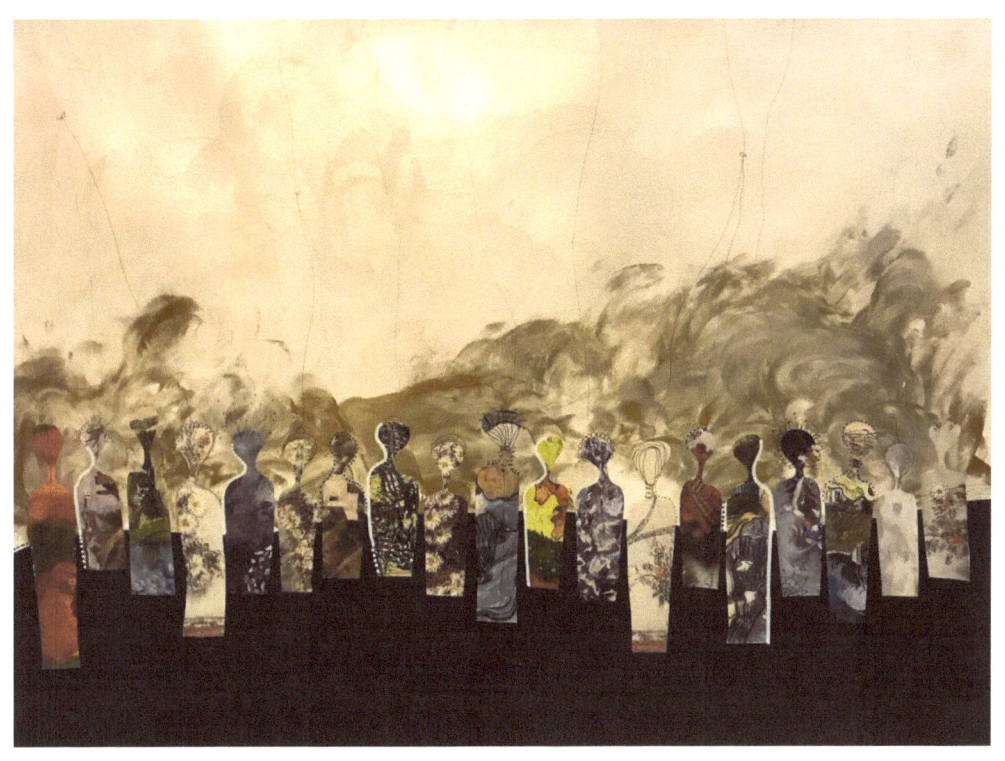

A Mist the Change; 2019; 19"x28"; mixed media on paper

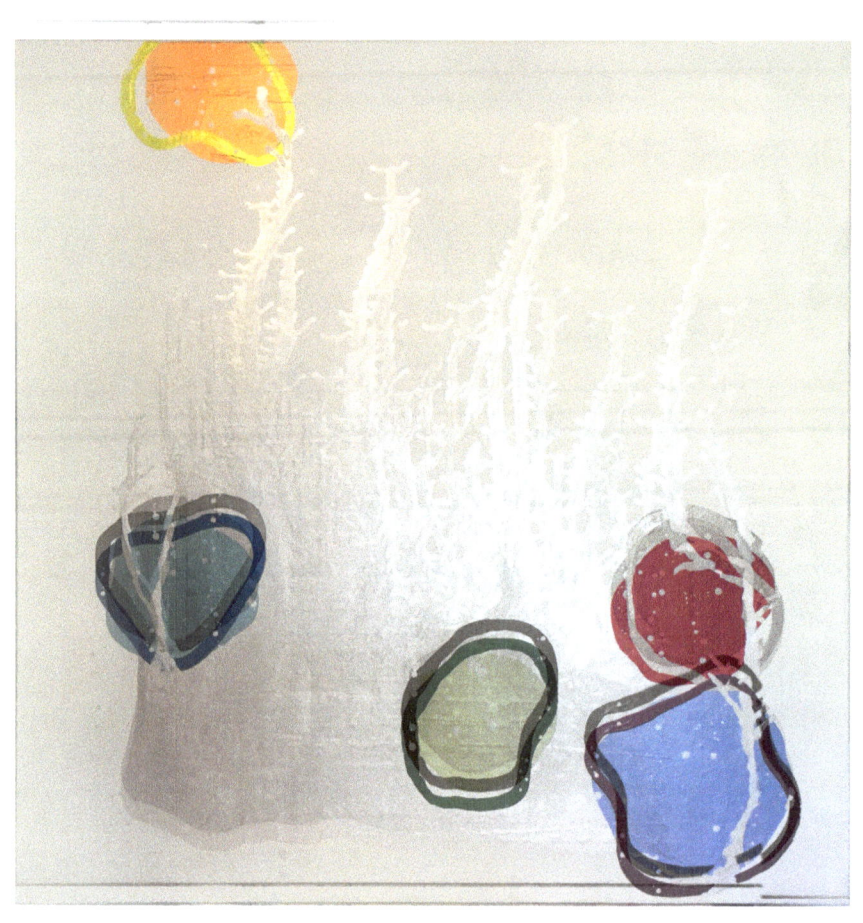

Elements; 2017; 48"x48"; acrylic on canvas

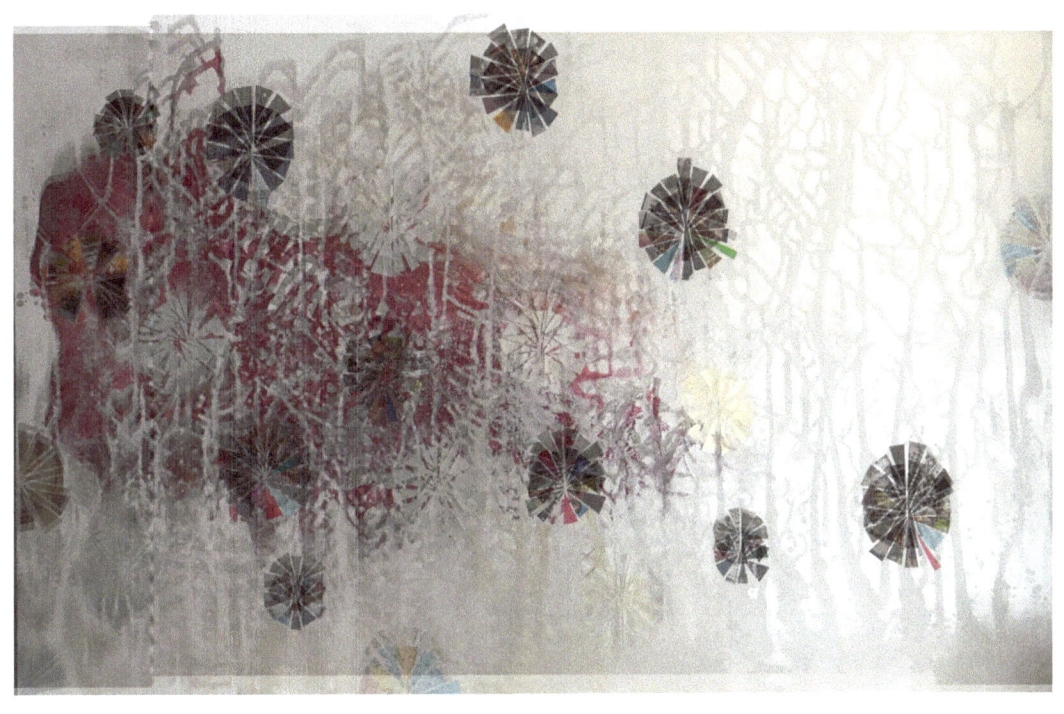

Zen Sunset; 2018; 36"x58"; acrylic, collage on canvas; (can be hung vertical or horizontal)

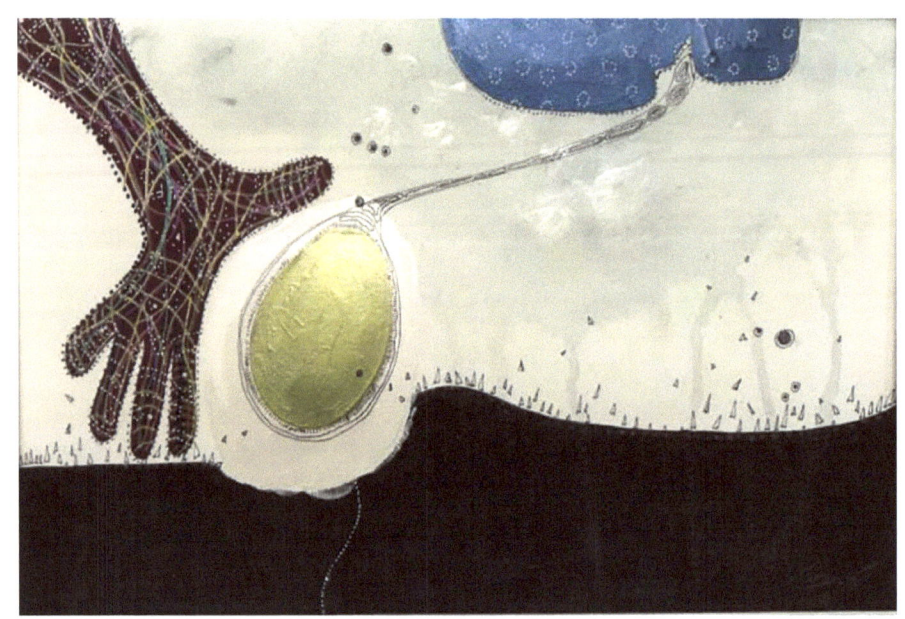

Growing Within; 2019; 9"x13"; mixed media on paper

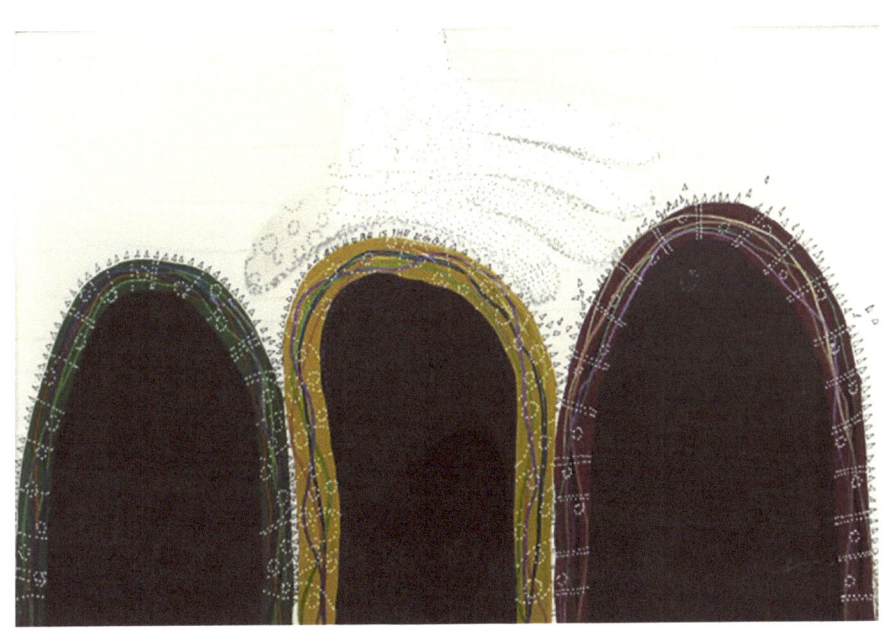

Where IS the Egg?; 2019; 9"x13"; mixed media on paper

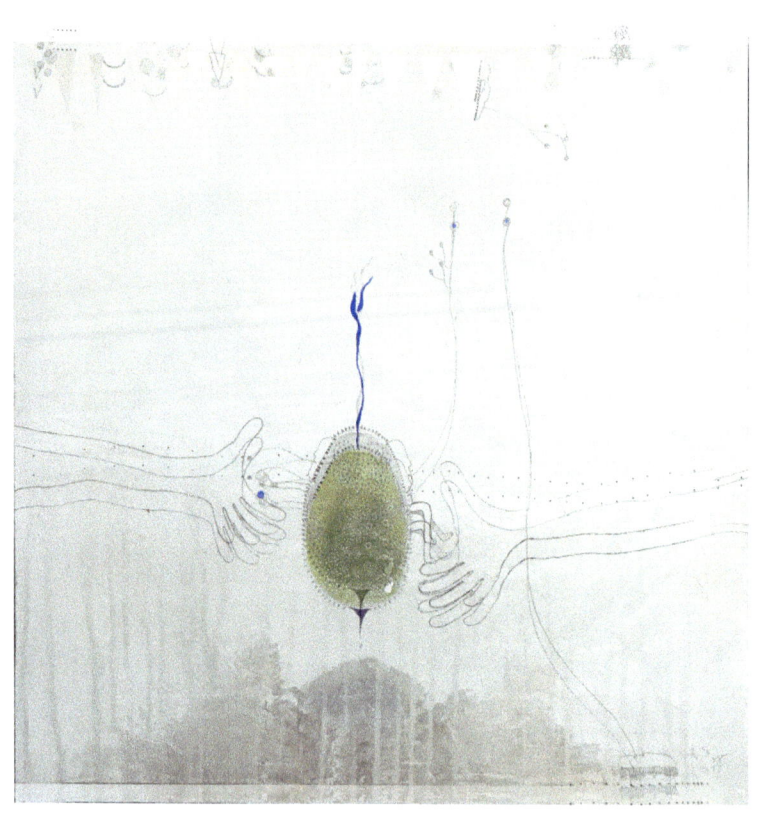

Cloud Egglas; 2019; 24"x24"; acrylic, ink on panel

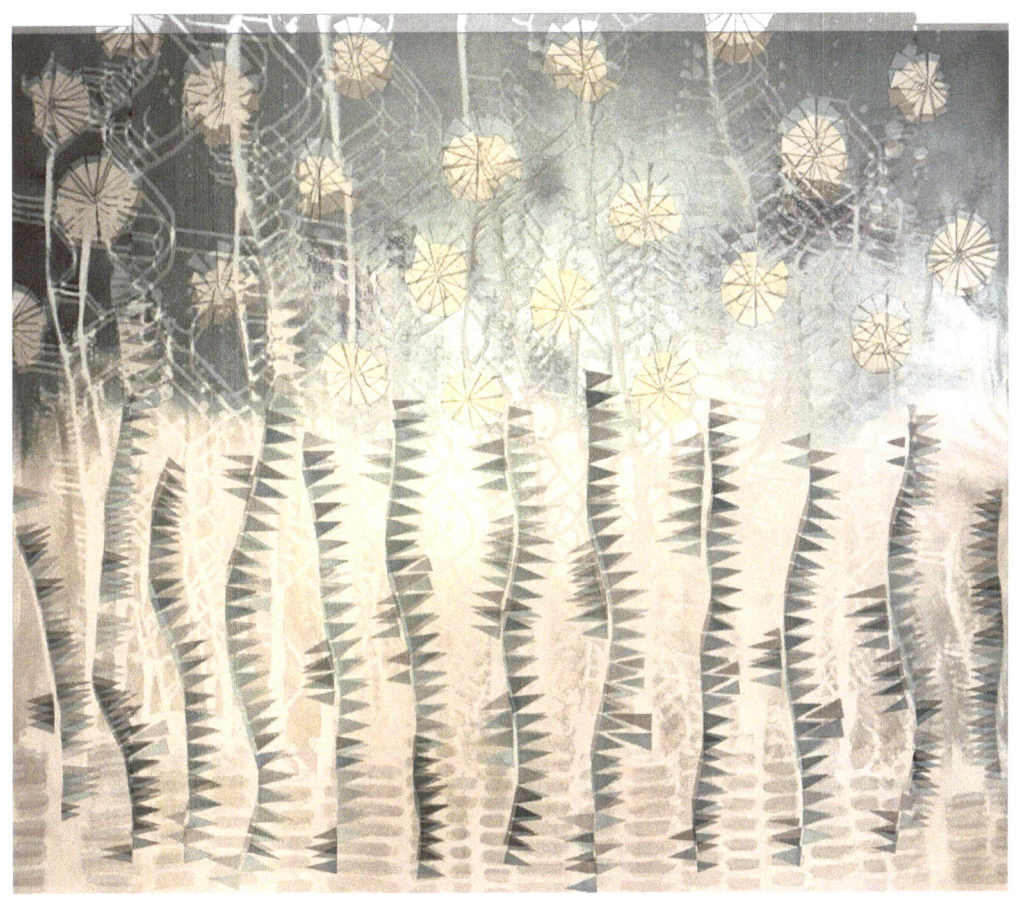

Blowing in the Wind; 2018; 48"x60"; acrylic, collage on canvas

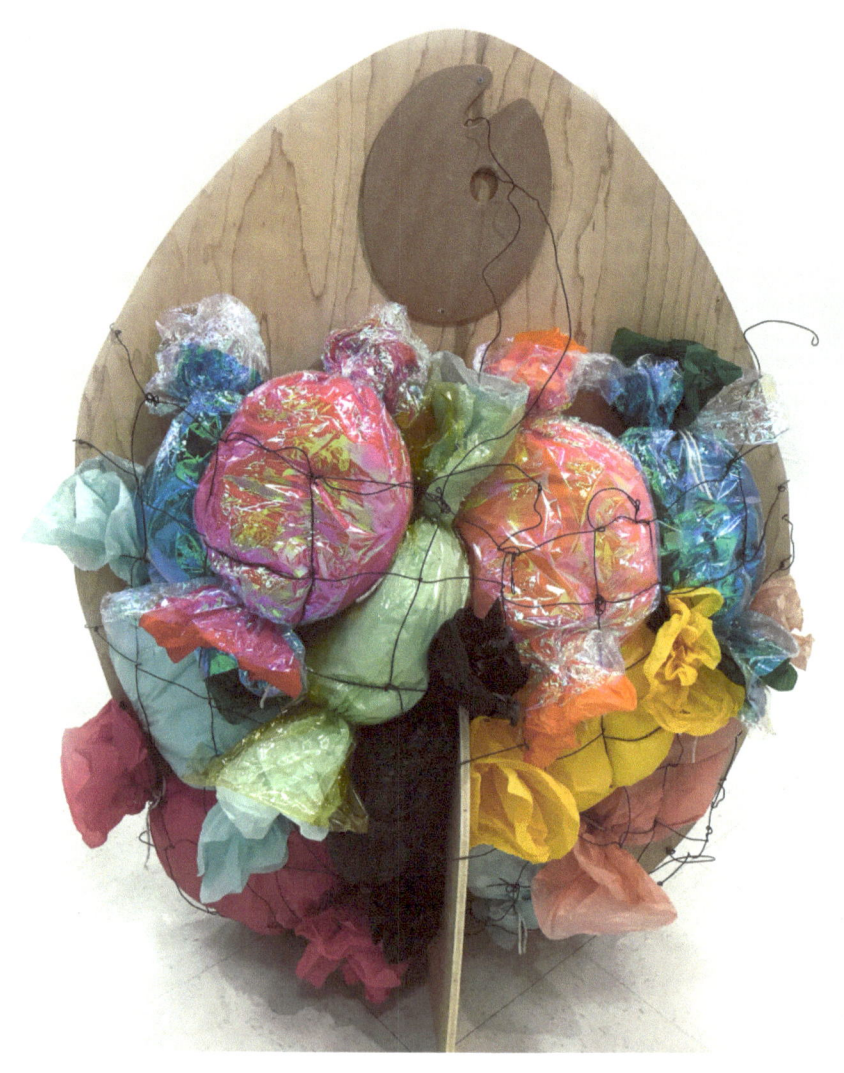

Eggs in a Basket; 2019; 4' x 37", wood, paper, pillow inserts

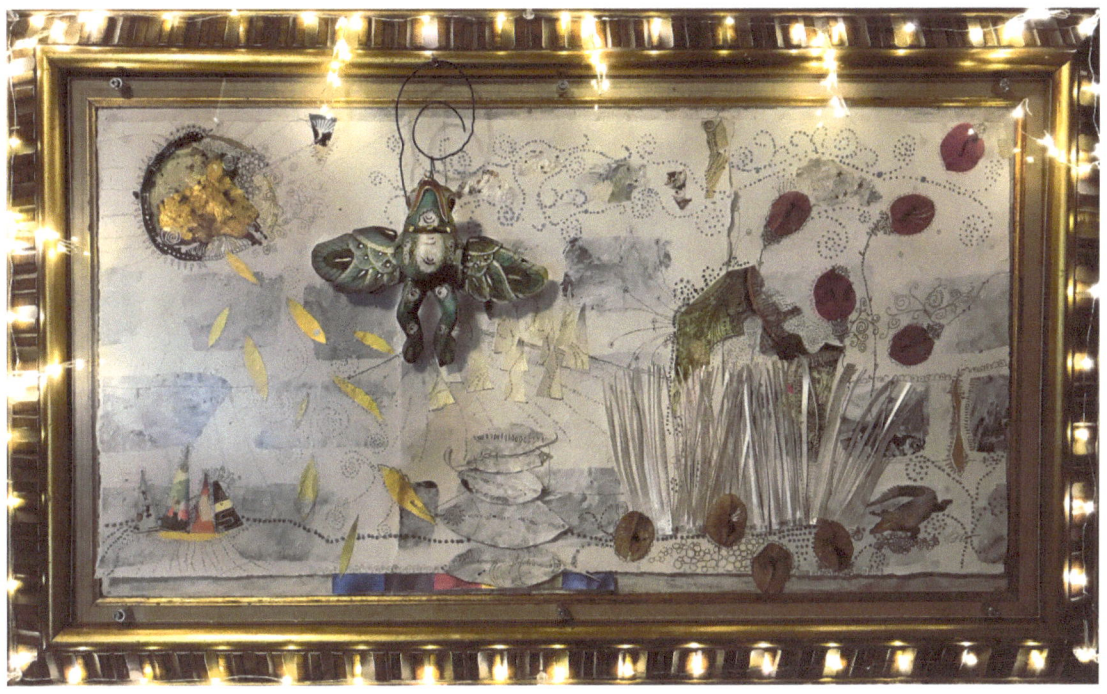

Your Stairway Lies in the Whispering Wind; 2019; 14"x30"/frame
22"x37"; mixed media on paper

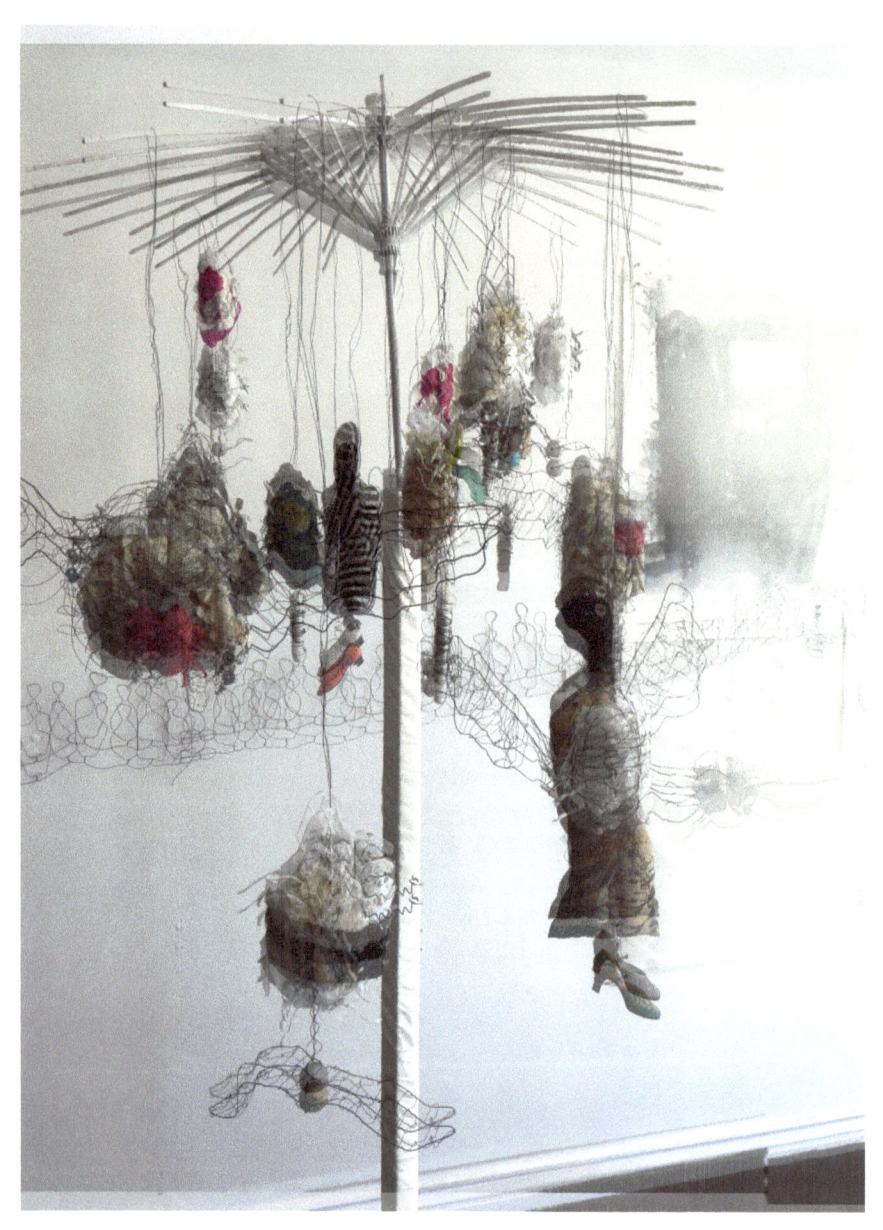

Tree of Hopes & Dreams; 2018; priced separately

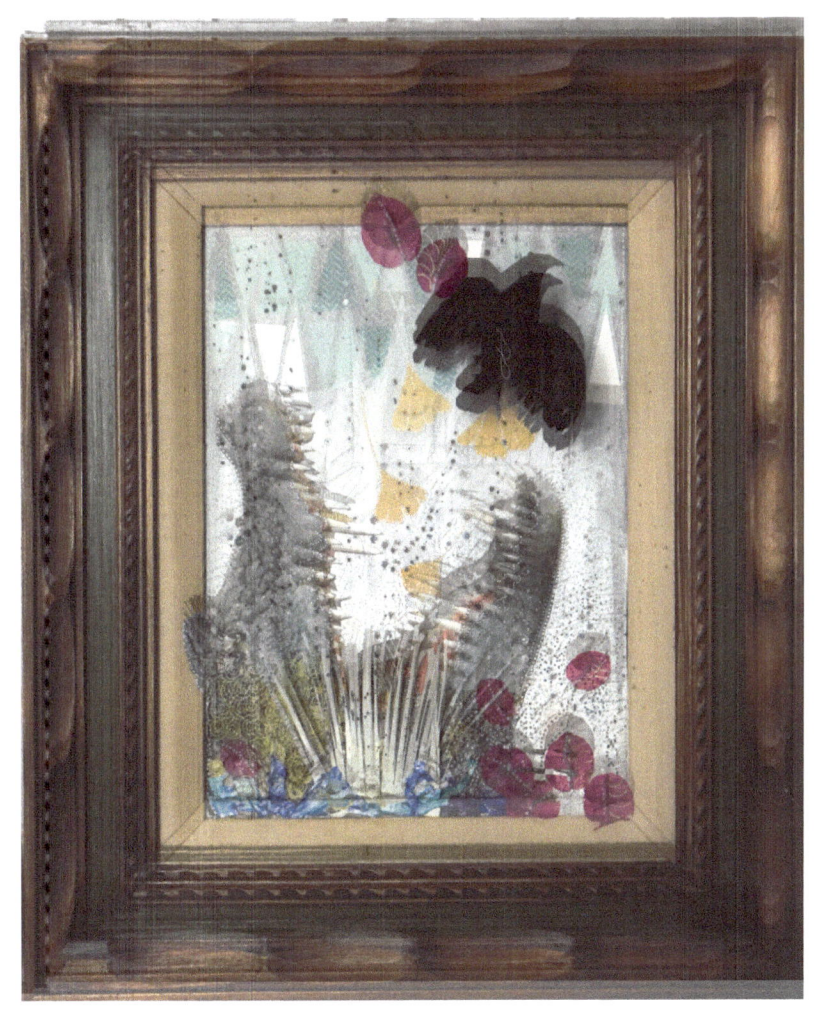

This Could Be Heaven or This Could Be Hell; 2019; 15"x11"/frame 24"x20"; mixed media on paper

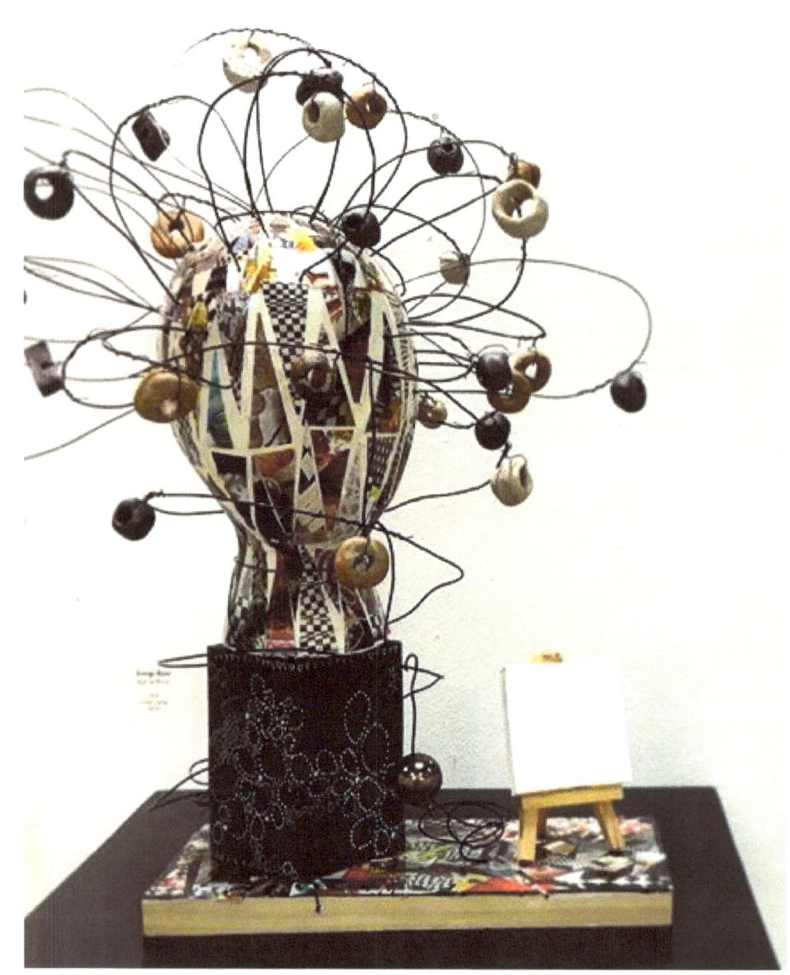

Energy Buzz; 2019; 20"x20"; mixed media

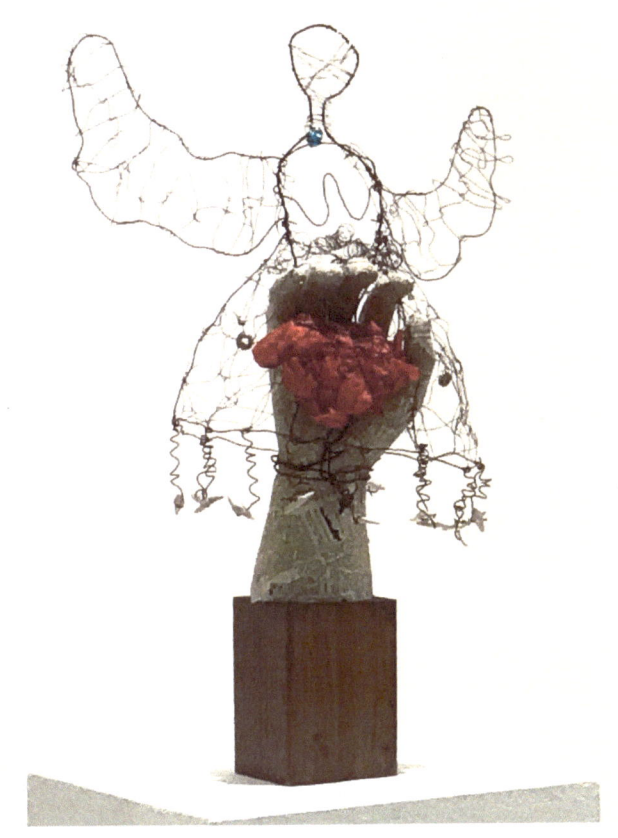

Heart in Hand; 2018; 20"x15"; wire, wook, plastic hand, collage

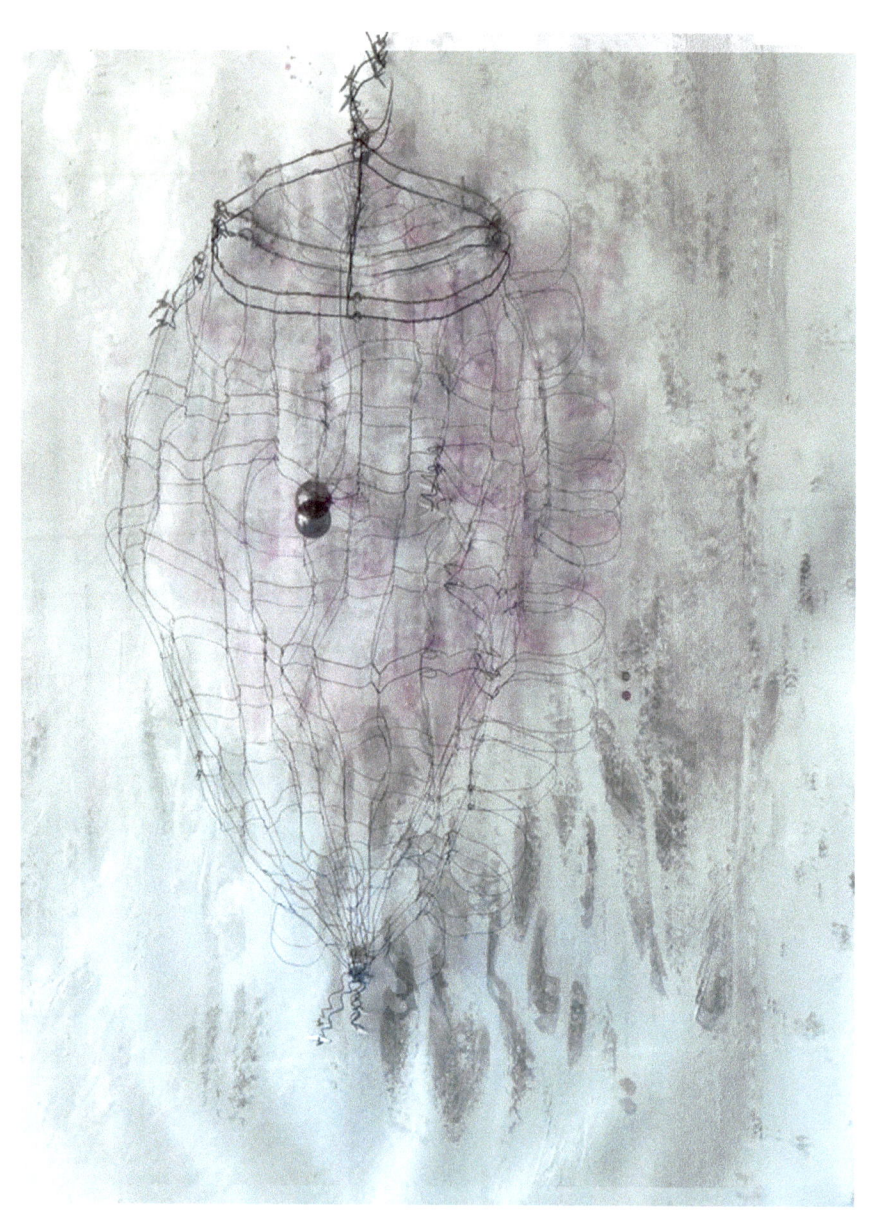

Cocoon Seedling; 2018; 44"x32"; mixed media on paper

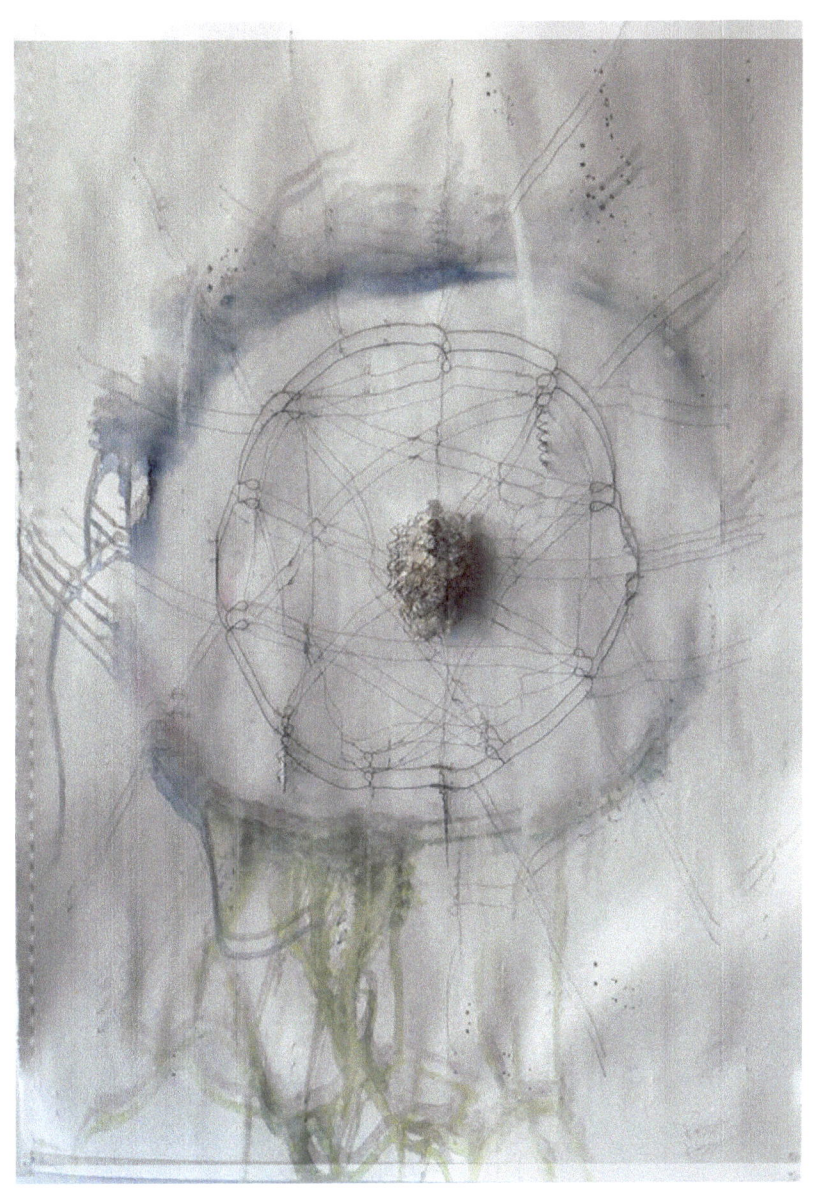

Protecting the Seeds of Hope; 2018; 44"x32"; mixed media on paper

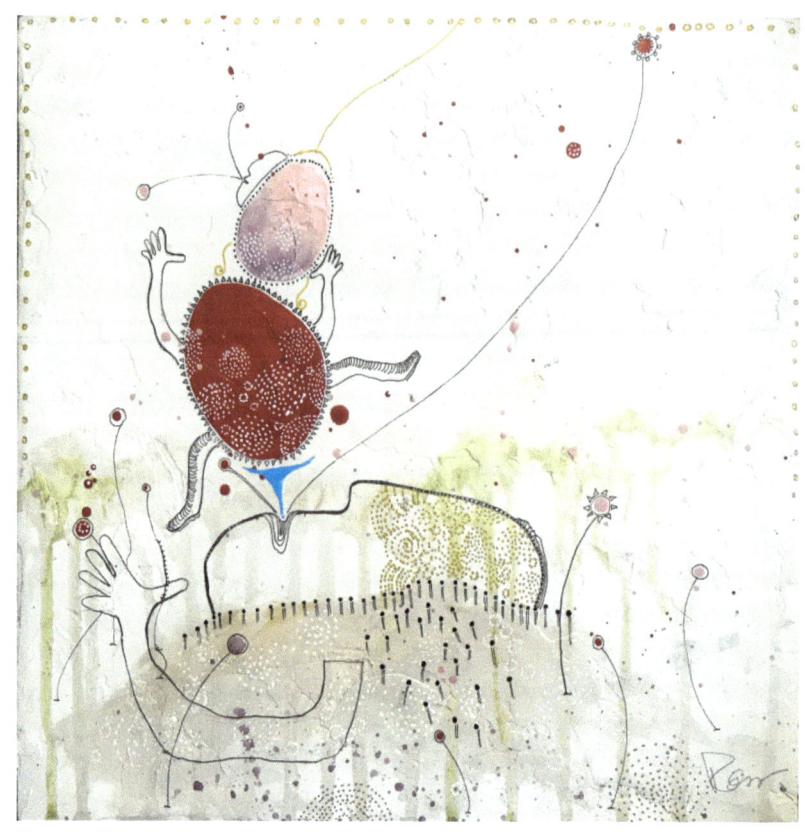

Jumping Off; 2019; 12"x12"; acrylic, ink on panel

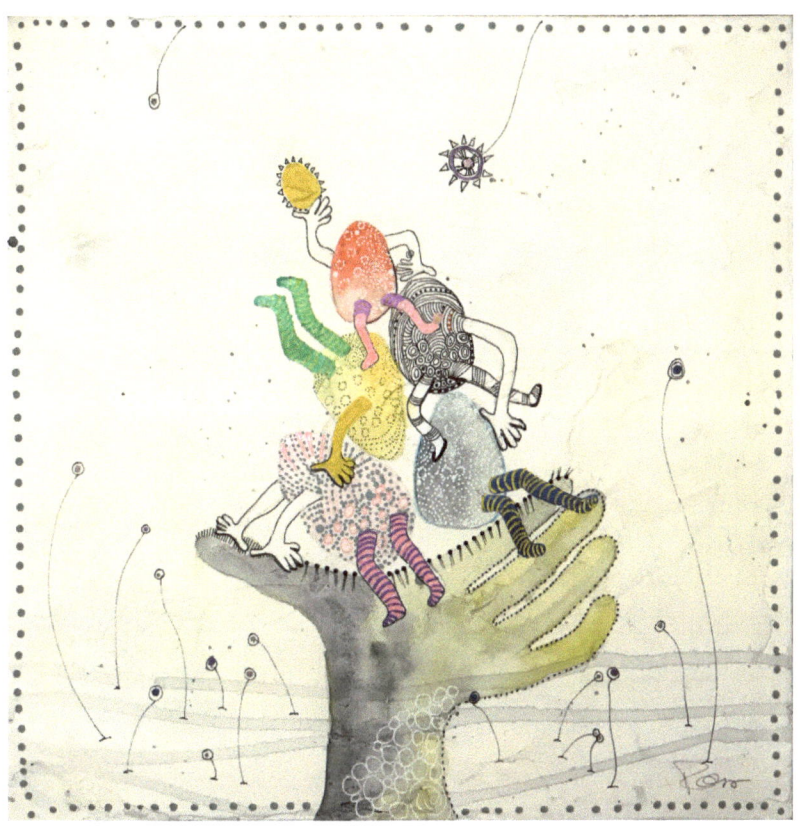

You Can Check Out Any Time You Like; 2019; 12"x12"; acrylic, ink on panel

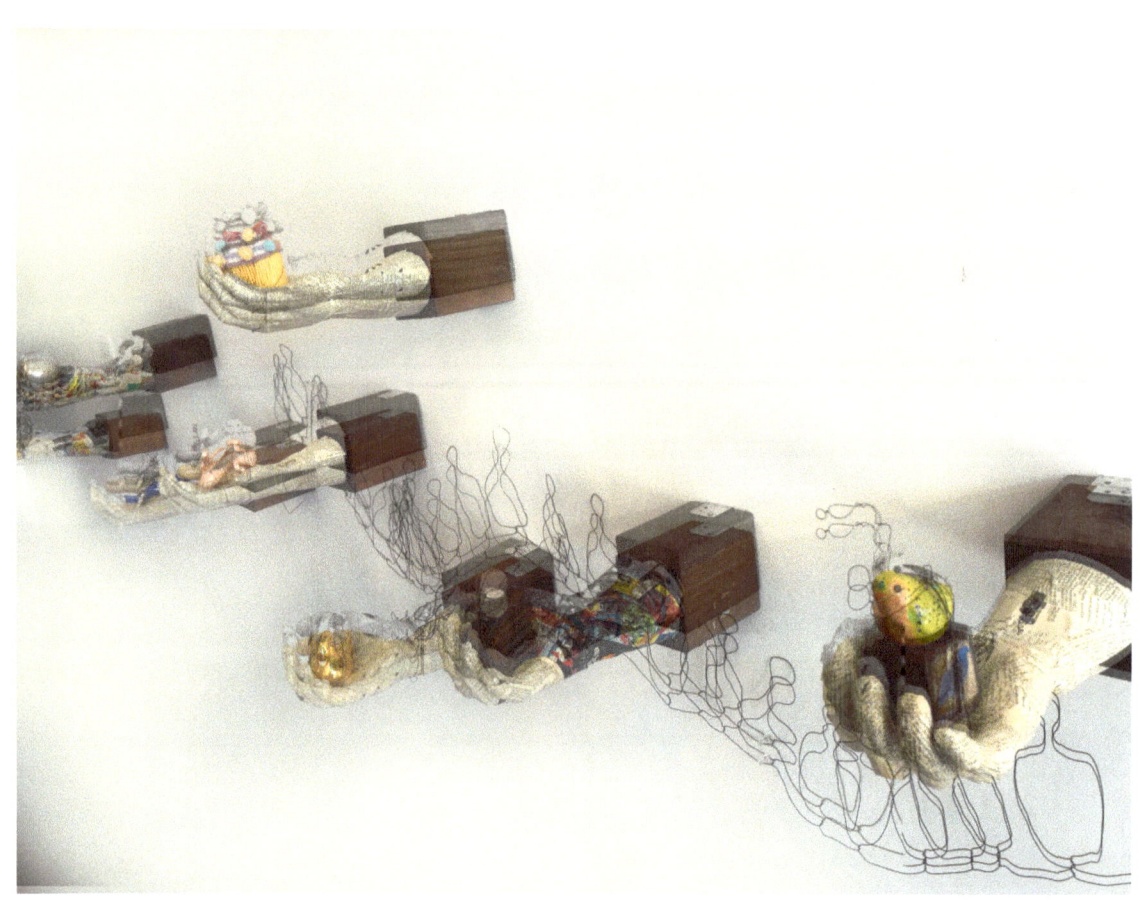

Gifts of Language; 2018; 4" x 4" x 15"-ish; each holding a different symbol; mixed media

Symbols Included: 1. heart, 2. wire and 3. solid energy ball, 4. flying hope, 5. ballet shoe, 6. golden duck, 7. ceramic bird, 8. blue fish, 9. Cupcake, 10: YOW

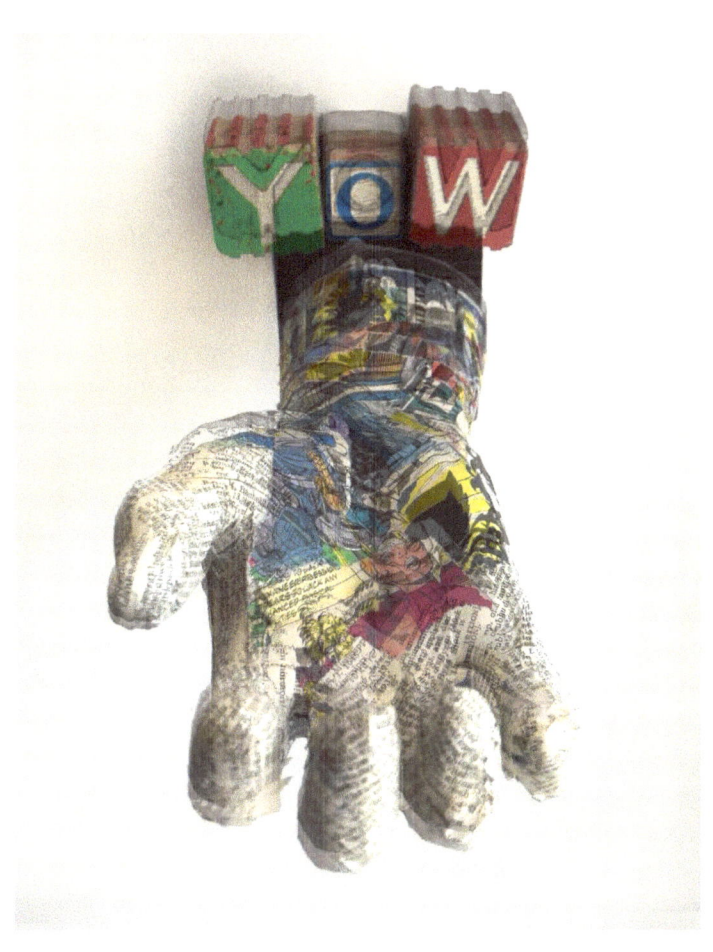
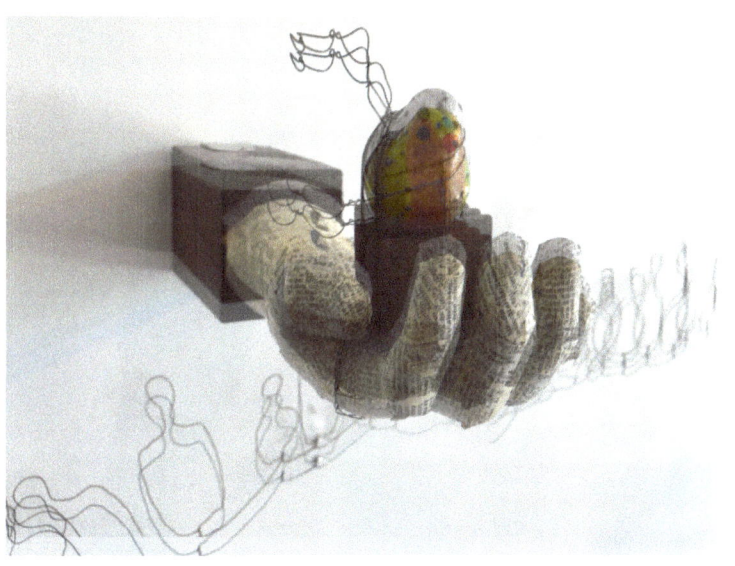

Artwork to be displayed at
the yearly fund raiser.

2019

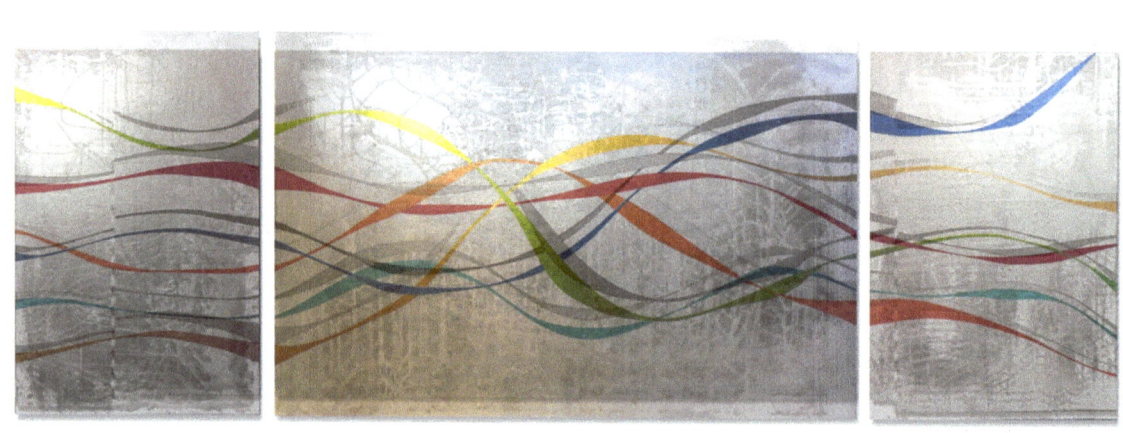

Waves of Distraction; 2017; 36"x106"; three pieces (2) 36"x24"; 36"x58"; acrylic on canvas

Karrie Ross :

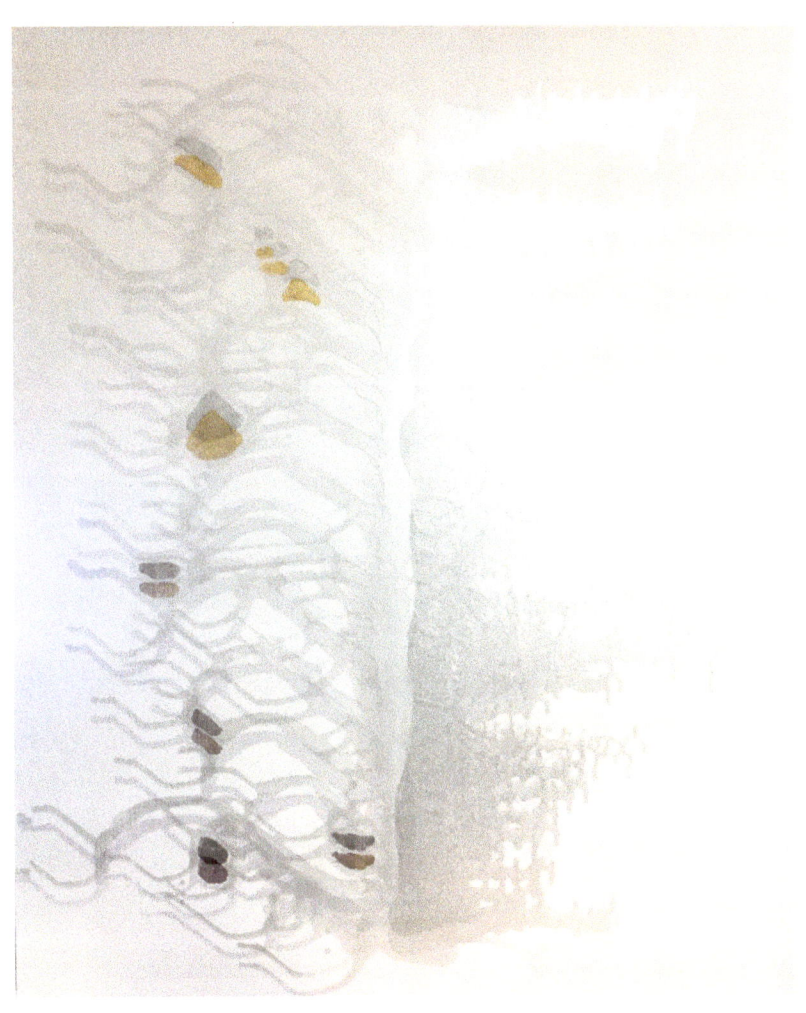

Crystal Ice; 2017; 58"x48"; acrylic on canvas; (can be hung vertical or horizontal)

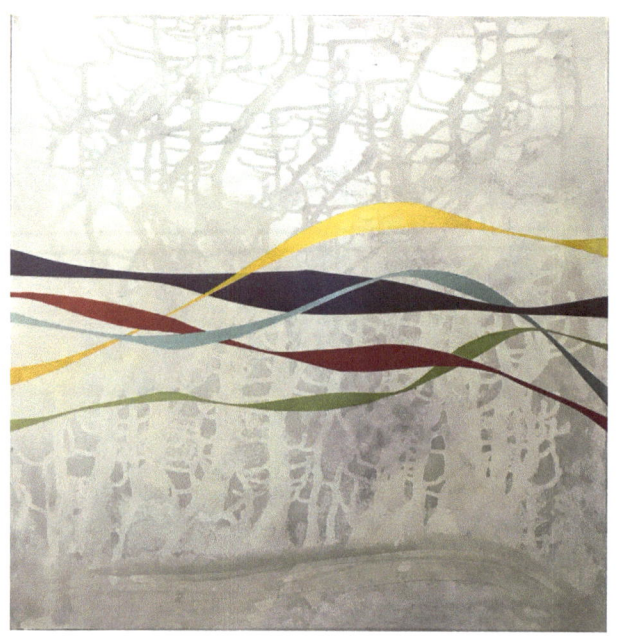 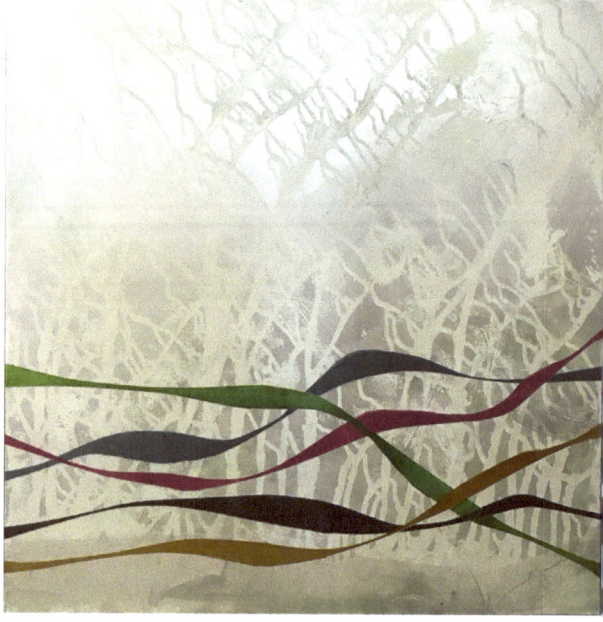

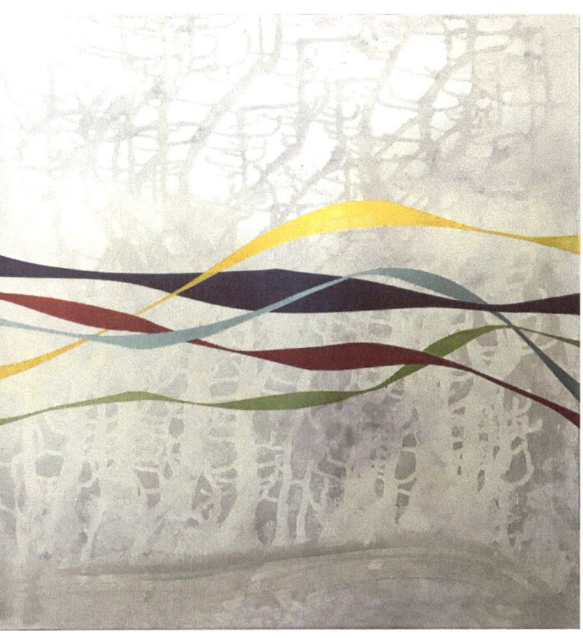
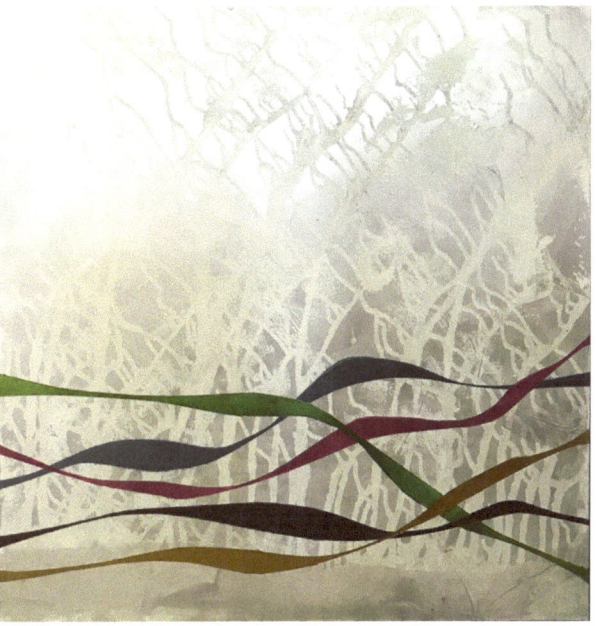

Whispering Waves; 2019; 4 panels each 36"x36"; vertical hang is 72"x72"; horizontal hang is 36"x144"; acrylic on canvas; (can be hung vertical or horizontal)

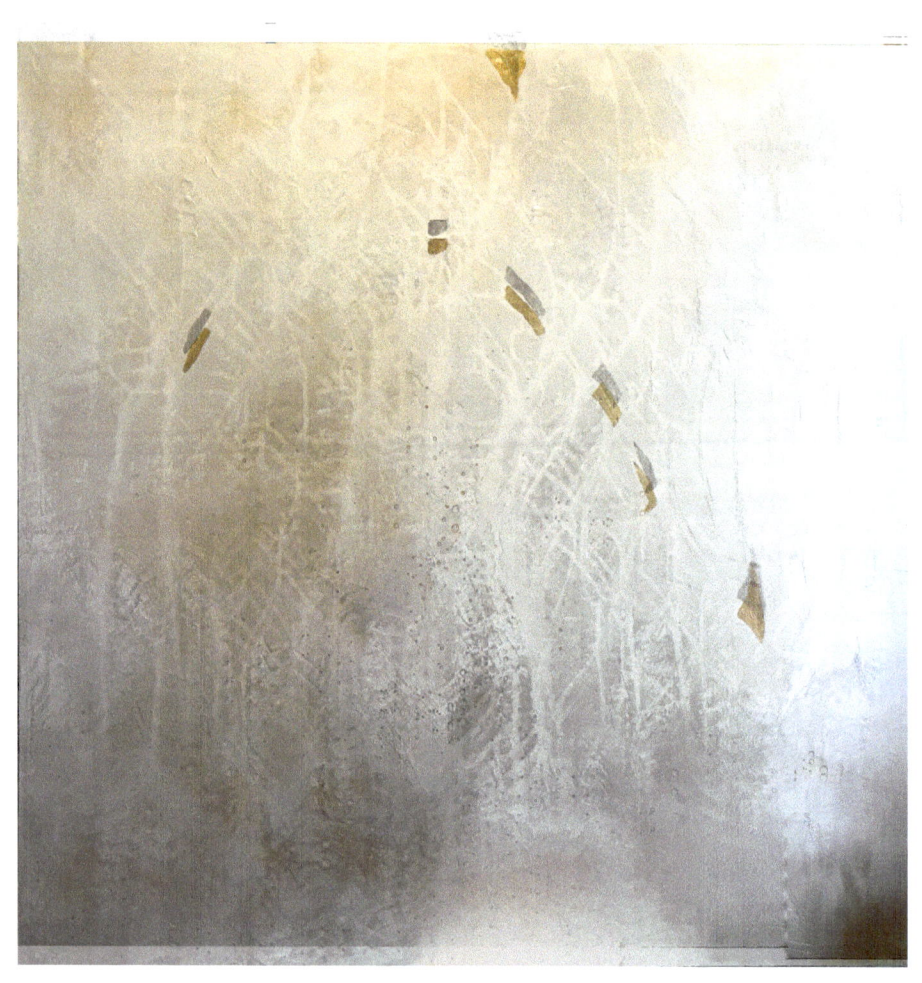

Golden Forest; 2018; 48"x48"; acrylic on canvas

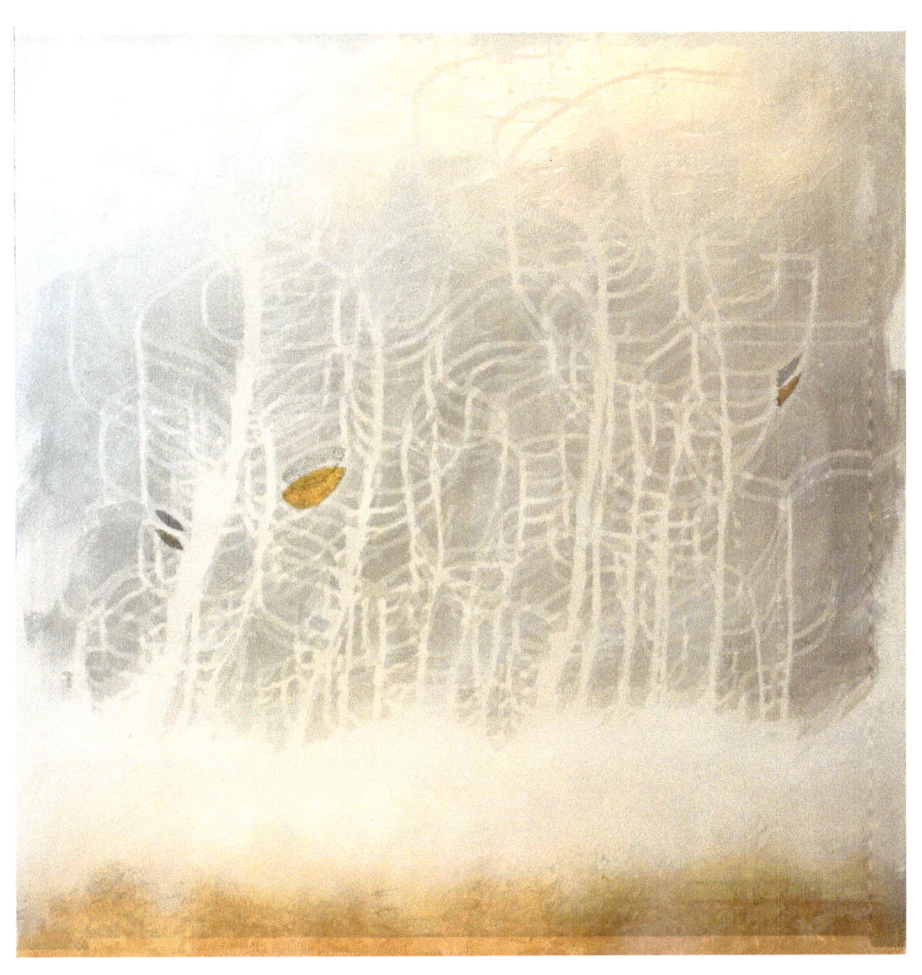

Golden Leaves; 2018; 48"x48"; acrylic on canvas

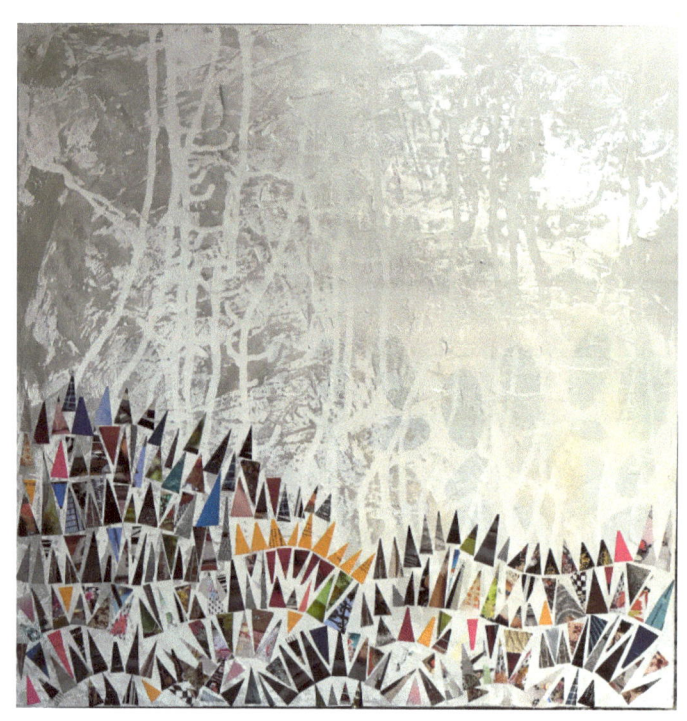

The Gathering; 2018; 30"x30"; acrylic, collage on canvas
On The Dawn; 2018; 30"x30"; acrylic, collage on canvas
Down in the Valley; 2018; 30"x30"; acrylic, collage on canvas

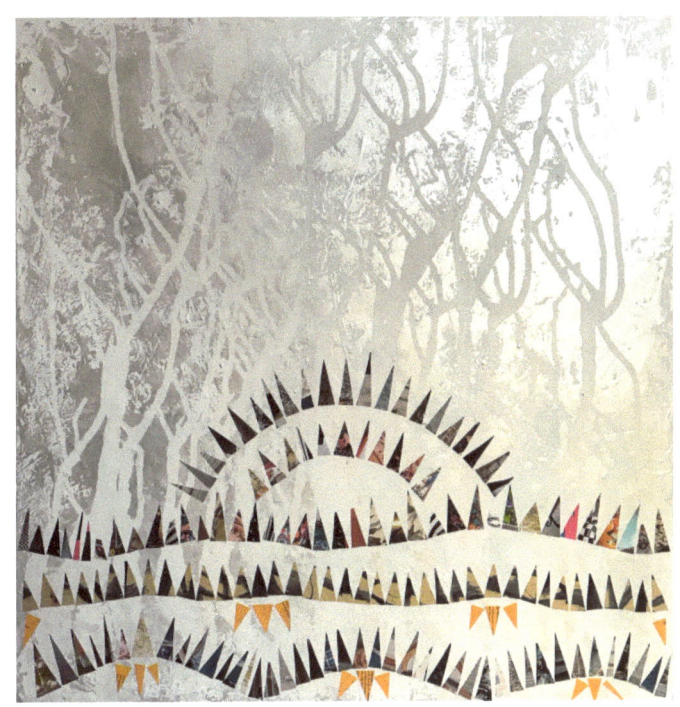
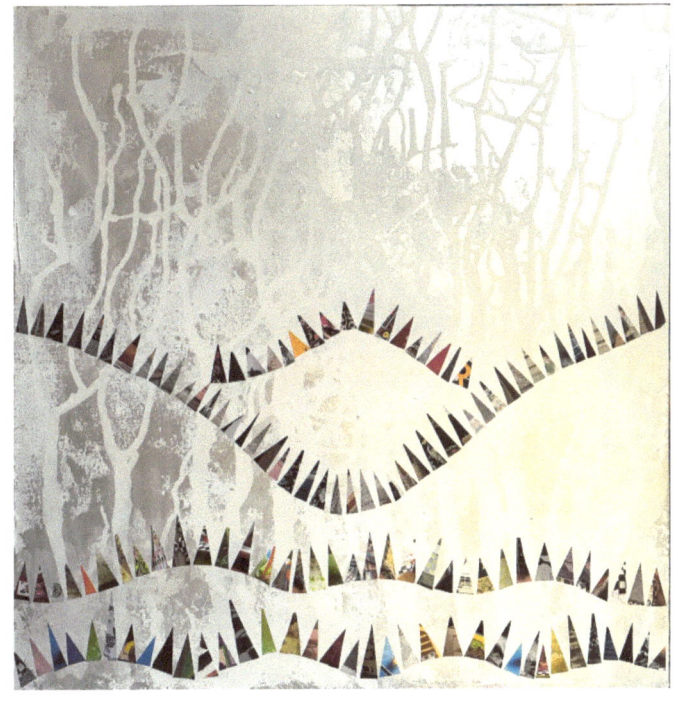

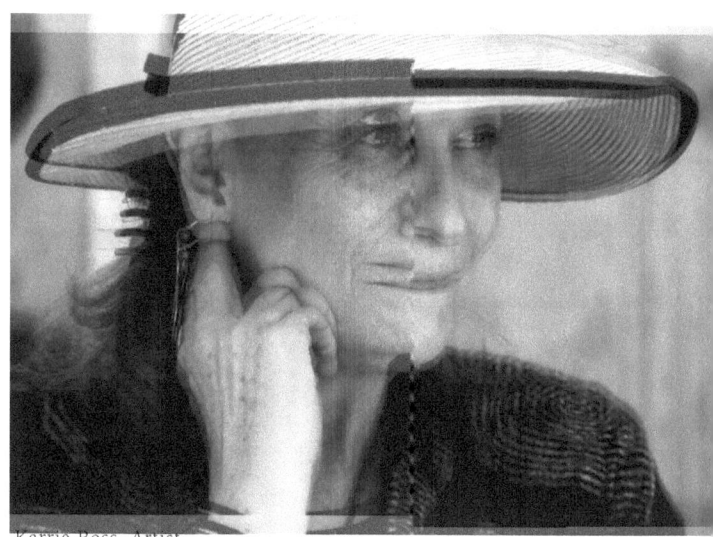

Karrie Ross, Artist

Biography

K arrie lives to affect energy

Karrie Ross is best known for her diverse use of mediums: wire, collage, acrylic-iridescent-minimalism-flow, pen & ink and watercolors. Ross' artwork grows out of a fascination with being human, the asking and answering of questions about the self in an intuitive manner, and bringing attention to the value of how one's energy affects living in this world. She calls it a "Collaboration with Nature".

A native to Los Angeles, with forty plus years of experience in her craft, she has a local and international collectors base. Her work was featured in over 170 exhibitions (since 2010), including museum shows at: the NYC Children's Museum of the Arts; Torrance Art Museum TAM; and a 6 month traveling exhibition beginning in Italy, next to the Oceanside Art Museum OAM; ending up at the Riverside Art Museum RAM; Los Angeles Municipal Art Gallery LAMAG; Kellogg University Gallery CalPoly; USC Keck School of Medicine Hoyt Gallery; San Diego Institute of Art as well as at galleries, non-profits, and project spaces around the Southern California area. Ross has also been highlighted in several publications including Hollywood Today, EasyReader, the Los Angles Times, USC online, and the Huffington Post. Apart from her art, Ross is also an award winning author and publishes a yearly art-project-book spotlighting artists 'in-life' stories, "Our Ever Changing World," Artist ART & Story, which focuses on creating community, and documenting the Art Scene in California, and internationally, over her life-time.

Ross currently lives and works in Los Angeles, California.

Remember this ... you are whole and complete just the way you are. Which really doesn't mean anything until you've taken the journey through the muck and survived—to go through more—with moments of light and great joy in between. With each new year I look forward to and live for the in betweens.

Karrie runs an award winning graphic design business (since 1996) that specializes in the design of fiction and non-fiction books, and collateral for self publishing authors, services, products and small businesses. She consults on brand recognition, promotion, marketing, merchandising, and on how to create a web-presence. She served on the Board of Directors for the Art Directors Club of Los Angeles for 5yrs in the 1980s, overseeing the Membership, Newsletter, and Public Relations committees.

www.KarrieRoss.com

Solo Exhibitions

– 2019 Blackboard Gallery, Studio Channel Islands: "Light&Space Through Time; the art of Karrie Ross"; Camarillo, CA
– 2019: Korean Cultural Center, "4 Artists: Nature, Line, Life, Los Angeles, CA
– 2018 Tieken Gallery, "Uncharted Encounters", Chinatown, CA
– 2018 FM Fine Art Gallery, "Vignettes: an exhibition of sight, being human, and hope", Los Angeles, CA
– 2017 Mike Kelly Gallery, "The Nature of Things", Venice, CA
– 2015 FMFine Art Gallery; "Kimono", Los Angeles, CA
– 2014 LA Artcore Union Center for the Arts; "Impact of Life", Los Angeles, CA

Select Museum/College/NonProfit Exhibitions

– ArtShareLA; "Drawn Together" 2017, group show curated by Mike Kelley
– Torrance Art Museum: 2016 South Bay Focus; Annual Curator, Peter Frank
– Los Angeles Municipal Gallery; Barnsdale Park, 2016 Annual Exhibition; Scott Canty
– Chaffey Community Museum; Curated; Riverside, CA
– MOAH/Cedar Lancaster: "Waterworks 1", Traveling show. Curator Juri Koll; Ojai, CA
– Los Angeles Municipal Art Gallery, Barnsdale Park, 2015 Annual Exhibition; Los Angeles, CA
– Three part Traveling International Museum Show (2014-2015) "California Dreaming" An International Portrait of Southern California. My artwork "Big and Small California Dreaming" curators have selected approximately 50 artworks from nearly one thousand entries. Curators; Peter Frank, Daniel Foster, Alfio Borghese. The exhibition will be seen at the following venues:
• Palazzo della Provincia di Frosinone, Frosinone, Italy; October, 2014
• Oceanside Museum of Art, OMA, Oceanside CA; December, 2014-2015
• Riverside Art Museum, RAM, Riverside, CA; May, 2015

– Kellogg University Art Gallery: "INK & CLAY 2014 & 2015 & 2017"; Curated; Pamona, CA
– Glendale College Gallery: "Waterworks 2", 2015, by VICA; traveling show. Curator Juri Koll
– MOAH Lancaster: Annual Curated Show; 2013; Lancaster, CA
– The Brand Library : "Works on Paper #25, #30 and #42"; Curator for #42: Jack Rutberg, Glendale, CA

Art Fairs

– 2018: The Other Art Fair by Saatchi Art: Art Fair Los Angeles, CA
– 2017: Pasadena Showcase House of Design; Fresh Paint Art Advisory
– LA Art Show; SCAA Sergott Contemporary Art Alliance ; Los Angeles, CA
– 2016: Dwell On Design, Fabrik, Los Angeles, CA
– World Wide Art Fair, Art Unified, Los Angeles, CA
– 2015: LA Art Show 2015: Fabrik Booth; Los Angeles, CA
– 2014: Dwell Lofts; DTLA, MaryLinda Moss

Installations

– Artist Residency at the Brewery Lofts, 1-Month interactive installation, at Shoebox Projects space. "Got Shui? A moment with Karrie Ross".
– ArtBasil-LA 2016; installation of mini booth, one among 40 who participated.
– City of Redondo Beach; CA 101 2017, 2016, 2015; located in the Redondo Beach; installs and 2D artwork.
– Mike Kelley Gallery: PODs the Crowd dynamic #1 "Inclusion/ Exclusion/Socialization; Venice, CA
– Art Project Book and Pop-up #1: "Our Ever Changing World: Through the Eyes of Artists": "What are you saving from extinction?"; Book Signing and Art Exhibit; group 36 artists in the book; Los Angeles, CA. This project is now on it's 12th book and growing.

Select List Gallery Group Exhibitions

2019
– Room & Board; group show; Culver City, CA
– Susan Eley Fine Art; "On The Rocks"; New York, NY
– Korean Cultural Center; "4 Artists: Nature, Line, Life" Los Angeles, CA; juror Susan Gray, Max Presneill
– USC Keck School of Medicine, Hoyt Art Gallery; "Artist & Researcher #3", Los Angeles, CA
– Coastline Community College Art Gallery "Kitsch In Sync"; Newport Beach CA, curator Bradford Salamon

2018 (selected list, I had an accident in May that caused me to withdraw to heal)
– Children's Museum of the Arts, NYC; "And Justice for Some"; traveling Show; New York, NY
– Room & Board; group show; Culver City, CA
– Arena 1 / WCA Women's Caucus for the Arts: "Art Speaks! Lend Your Voice"; group show; Juror Jillith Moniz; Santa Monica, CA
– Mike Kelley Gallery "The Four of Us"; group show; Venice, CA
– Orange County Center for Contemporary Art (OCCCA) : "Music For Your Eyes"; group show; Juror Peter Frank, Santa Ana, CA

2017
– Art & Home: Room and Board/Angeleno magazine "An evening with Los Angeles Family Housing"; Curator Trina Churchill; Culver City, CA
– SoLA: "FRESH"; jurors Fatemeh Burnes, Peter Frank
– SFAC San Francisco: "And Justice for Some"; traveling Show; invited by "Walter Maciel Gallery"
– Walter Maciel Gallery: "And Justice for Some"; traveling Show; invited to participate

2016
– MuzeuMM: FAUXisn: DADA Reconstructed; Curator Kio Griffith; group show, Los Angeles, CA
– Art & Home: Art & Home/ Angeleno magazine "An evening with Los Angeles Family Housing"; Curator Trina Churchill; Culver City, CA
– Chaffey Community Museum; Old Broads 2; Ontario, CA
 South Bay Contemporary: "Skyline": Curator: Ben Zask; San Pedro, CA
– BG Gallery: Summer Show; Bergamot Station, Santa Monica
– Angels Ink: "imagine that": Curator: Robin Hinchliffe; San Pedro, CA

2015
– Porch Gallery; WaterWorks II: Curators: Peter Frank, Juri Koll, Lisa Casoni, Heather Stobo, John Yau. Ojai, CA
– Gallery Antenna: "Homing Pigeon : Edition 4: Kyoto" - traveling show; curator Kio Griffith; Kyoto, Japan
– Wilding Cran: "Bunnymania"; National Museum of Animals and Society fund raiser. Curator Peter Frank, Los Angeles, CA
– The San Diego Art Institute: MAS Attack 8; Group show, San Diego, CA
– Loft as Liz's: Waterworks I; Curator Juri Koll, VICA; Sam Francis Foundation ; Traveling show; Los Angeles, CA
– BG Gallery: Grayscale Wonderland; Bergamot Station, Santa Monica
– BG Gallery: 144 Show; Bergamot Station, Santa Monica
– The Atrium: Line in Motion; curator Jill Thayer, Paso Robles, CA

2014
– Porch Gallery: Venice Institute of Contemporary Arts; "Water Works": Traveling show. Curator Juri Koll, Ojai, CA
– Studio C Gallery: Santa Fe Arts Colony: "Oneira: I Dream the Self"; Juror: Betty Brown; Los Angeles, CA
– Topanga Canyon Gallery; Annual Show; AWARD Third Place; Juror: Jim Morphesis. Topanga, CA

2013
– Bleicher/Golightly/Gorman: "From Little Things Big Things Grow"; Santa Monica, CA
– Broadway Art Space:Group Show: "Women Make the World Go Round"; Santa Monica, CA
– The Peace Project 2013; Whole-9; one of 165 pieces for a traveling show. Culver City, CA
– Red Pipe Gallery: "City & Self"; Curator Mat Gleason; Los Angeles, CA
– Garboushian Gallery: "MANA" Fundraiser: Curator Lori Garboushian; Beverly Hills, CA

2012
– The Peace Project 2012; Honorable mention; Whole-9; Traveline Show, Culver City, CA
– LAX, Terminal 1: "Le Petite Jardin"; Los Angeles, CA – 6mons install
– Billboard Art in two Cities: Reading, PA, and Corona, CA

2011
– Chicago Billboard Project: Ten images with the words, "Breast Awareness". Chicago, Ill
– Pacific Art League: National Competition, Juror: JoAnne Northrup, San Jose Museum of Art, Palo Alto, CA
– Gallery 825: Annual Auction; "Oh The Two Of Us" SOLD to Mr. and Mrs. Herair Garboushian; Los Angeles, CA
– Gallery 825: "Not A Car"; Jurors: Silvia Sonnenschmidt and Thomas Volkmann; Los Angeles, CA

2010
– Blossoms II Award Show: AWARD: Honorable Mention awarded to Spiral Series: Energy Blooms: "We Dance"; selected from 2,300 entries; Susan Kathleen Black Foundation
– Williams-Sonoma Home; Fall Wall Decor: "Graffiti"
– TAG Gallery, "California Open" Bergamot Station; Juror: Karen Moss; Santa Monica, CA
– Santa Monica Cultural Affairs; Annenberg Beach House; Santa Monica, CA
– The Brewery Art Walk; Los Angeles, CA

1999-2008 Selected sales to the decorative industry through a gallery at High Point, Atlanta, GA
2009 The Brewery Art Walk, Los Angeles, CA
2001 United Way: 'The Pier' on permanent display at corporate offices Los Angeles, CA

Curatorial Exhibitions
– FM Fine Art Gallery: "Echo"; Los Angeles, CA
– Beyond Baroque: "Nature Within"; Venice, CA
– South Bay Contemporary: "The FACES Within" curated by me show, San Pedro, CA
– "Our Ever Changing World: Through the Eyes of Artists": Artists/Art/Story; Book Signing for 90 artists in the book; Los Angeles, CA
– FM Fine Art Gallery: "My Own Private Moon"; Los Angeles, CA
– FM Fine Art Gallery: "Unexpected Dialogues" featuring for Mike Street and Jim O'Neil
– FM Fine Art Gallery: "LINE" featuring Jill Sykes, Emily Elise Halpern, Beanie Kamen; Los Angeles, CA
– "Our Ever Changing World: Through the Eyes of Artists": Couples and Collaboration: One night event. Book Signing and Art Exhibit; group showing of all 24 artists in the book; Los Angeles, CA
– "Our Ever Changing World: Through the Eyes of Artists": One night event. Question: "What are you saving from extinction?"; Book Signing and Art Exhibit; group showing of all 36 artists in the book; Los Angeles, CA

LARGE "Art Happenings"
– Hauser Wirth & Schimmel: "Now Be Here"; group photo documenting Women Artists; Organized by Kim Schoenstadt; Los Angeles, CA - 2016
– Reykjavik Art Museum: Yoko Ono Project "Arising", Testament of Harm for Being a Woman; Tryggvagata - 2016
– Shoshana Wayne Gallery: "Chain Letter" curated by Christian Cummings & Doug Harvey; over 1,700 artists participated—it was truly an ART Happening; Santa Monica, CA - 2011

Grants / Residencies / Lectures / Workshops / Videos / Interviews
– Artist Residency at the Brewery Lofts, 1-Month, at Shoebox Projects space, Interactive Installation.
– Saddleback College; Interview/Q&A to art class with John Seed
– Riverside College; Guest lecture with Sharon Suhovy
– C-Suite Quarterly Magazine; Image spotlighted in Desirables section
– Artvoices Magazine; Cover and interview Fall issue, ad in Winter issue
– Online interview "Heroines Journey", Peter de Kuster

Awards, Affiliations, Collections, and Accolades
– "The Lung IS Pink", USC Keck School of Medicine Dr. E. David lung studies collection. 2019
– "Trees Talking" # ____; collection of Andi Campognone, 2014

- "Dances With Flowers"; Artist Portfolio Magazine: AWARD; Q1 Honorable mention
- "Spiral Series: Energy Bloom" subset won honorable mentions in two juried art award shows and one for the Blossoms II National show.
- The "Portraits" series, "Freedom" won an honorable mention in the 2012 Whole 9 Traveling Peace Project.
- "As the Cloud Weeps: Bejeweled Bird" won 3rd place; 2013, juror Jim Morphesis
- Ross is also an 3x award-winning author of a non-fiction book about Parenting, and wrote an award-winning children's book engaging environmental issues for her line of characters the Bebuddies.com

Alternative Exhibitions

More can be seen in fine and decorative art installations across the world; hotels in Japan; New York, and retail outlets such as: JDA, Macy's, FAO Schwartz, MayCo., Dillards, Sax Fifth Ave, Gladmans, Coach, JCPenney's, Khol's, FredMyers, AGI, Hirshbedner, etc. interior design showrooms like Baker Design at the PDC. Throughout the U.S. my fine art has also been seen on TV and cable shows CSI Miami, The Standoff, Entourage, Medium, Movies: Shadowboxer, Burn After Reading, etc.:

www.KarrieRoss.com